****

C L A S S   G U I D E

F O R

P H Y S I C A L   E D U C A T I O N

****

CLASS GUIDE FOR PHYSICAL EDUCATION

****

by

William A. Groves, Ph. D.
Coordinator of Graduate Studies
Eastern Illinois University
Charleston, Illinois

and

J. H. Griffin, M. S.
Former Director of Physical Education
Teutopolis Community Unit High School
Teutopolis, Illinois

****

SCHOOL AID COMPANY
DANVILLE, ILLINOIS
1968

iv

FOREWORD

It is the purpose of this book to serve as a guide and source book in the general field of physical education particularly on the upper elementary and secondary level. Also,

To provide simple and workable plans for the administration and instruction of physical education under many differing types of facilities and personnel.

To allow for a flexibility that will adapt itself to various seasonal and regional interests.

To meet the general goals as set up by authoritative physical education people, yet permitting the class instructors to express their individuality and judgment in all phases of the program within the general plan.

To stimulate the readers of this book to adapt and add to the ideas contained herein and to so strengthen their program that it becomes custom made for the locale in which it is being applied.

To aid in giving a professional tone to the content and conduct of the physical education classes.

To provide challenging sporting activities for the _average_ boy, who may have good coordination, but still not be able to get the recognition that varsity participation would give in a major sport.

To help the physical education student who is still in school and who aspires to be a teacher in this worthwhile field formulate a plan of action.

Finally, to help him develop for himself a philosophy that will strengthen him in the desire to stay in the field and do what he can to give it the constant improvement it will always need.

PREFACE

This book is properly titled a CLASS GUIDE FOR PHYSICAL EDUCATION. It is to be used as a compass, but the instructor must be the captain and determine the directions the course will take. The material presented is presumed to be used by educators who have been trained professionally in the basic concepts of physical education, or those who are students and hope to enter the field of physical education. It is designed for boys in the 13 to 20 year age group, though flexible enough to be helpful for all ages.

Whenever possible, long discourses in any subject area have been avoided. The format of the CLASS GUIDE was chosen in order that the book may be used as a source book, a guide, and is so planned that the user may inject his own ideas and variations.

Every community is different, and the students' interests change with their environment. A good physical education program must meet the needs of the individuals concerned. Large classes tend to force the instructor to pour his classes into one mold and may make all participate in the same activity at the same rate of progress. We hope that this GUIDE will aid in setting up a flexible program that will meet individual needs, climatic conditions, community interests, and of course, not be in conflict with sound modern thinking about physical education.

The authors suggest that the many lesson plans be varied to meet the local situation. To test, teach, and re-test is a good procedure in the academic classroom and just as sound in the gymnasium. Much of the material in this handbook has already been called to your attention through college classes, personal experience in the field, or outside reading and observation. We hope that our plan paves the way for an improved program of physical education.

Ample room has been provided, particularly in the CLASS GUIDE section, for the instructor to add his own notes for variations to meet his needs. We feel, however, that we have in this GUIDE a vehicle that will fit most time schedules and any size work area. We feel, too, that it will stimulate dozens of ideas for coping with unexpected emergencies. Many such emergencies can leave the instructor with fifty students, twenty minutes, and only a small empty classroom in which to work. Emergency assemblies that take over the normal area for gym classes occur too frequently, and when they do occur, the instructor will have to "roll with the punch" and improvise. It might also be cold and raining outside, thereby forcing you to use whatever space is available inside.

In the interest of saving space the material has been tabulated whenever possible. If the instructor follows the five point program indicated on all class guides, he will do a creditable job that will yield the greatest results and benefits for his students.

TABLE OF CONTENTS

CHAPTER   I.

F I V E   P A R T   P E R I O D

1. Roll   Call

2. Activity   Preparation

3. Related   Activity   Commentary

4. The   Activity

5. Dismissal

Physical Education Objectives

To provide experience in leadership.

To provide an opportunity for all to excel in some activity.

To become acquainted with many competitive activities.

To develop habits of punctuality.

To learn to appreciate a healthy body.

To learn good health practices.

To learn at least elementary first aid.

To learn that good sportsmen can be gentlemen.

To learn the care and function of the principal parts of the body.

To develop wholesome attitudes.

To increase physical endurance and muscular strength.

To provide contests involving bodily contact.

To teach observance of the rules of the game.

To teach loyalty to a team.

To provide wholesome outlets for the emotions.

To foster and develop friendships.

To teach the acceptance of reasonable discipline necessary for the good of the group.

To recognize the need for self-discipline in order to achieve the greatest physical efficiency.

To_____

Each class period is made up of five activities:

1. <u>ROLL CALL</u>

There are many methods of determining the attendance. There might be a best and fastest way. The time saved may be used for more activity.

2. <u>ACTIVITY PREPARATION</u>

This is called by many the warmup period. It can and must be more. It should prepare the body for the stress to which it may be subjected during the class period. This might be three to seven minutes, or the goal may be to induce perspiration.

3. <u>RELATED ACTIVITY COMMENTARY</u>

Every period something specific and related to the student's needs should be taught. This might include game rules of the day, how to cut toenails, or activities outside of school, such as hunting or recreational pursuits. Anything over five minutes would tend to bore.

4. <u>THE ACTIVITY</u>

This should vary with the section of the country, and the interests and needs of the people involved. The instructor may use many assistants, possibly student assistants. Acquaint the class with many games, including the area's favorite one, and try to improve the necessary skills. The length of the ACTIVITY in each period will be the difference between the time used for sections 1, 2, 3, 5 and the allotted time for the class.

5. <u>DISMISSAL</u>

The shower period should be supervised. It insures the bath, prevents horseplay and the possible resulting injuries, and gives an opportunity to observe body impediments that might have escaped attention during medical examinations. The locker room check teaches good housekeeping and is appreciated by the maintenance men.

The section which follows enlarges on the five areas of the physical education period as presented in the CLASS GUIDES. Read them; then, use the margins for your notes, and, you may end up with a manual that for your situation will be the best one ever made.

1. ROLL CALL

The period between the ringing of the bell of the class preceding the time allotted for physical education and the actual calling of the roll is important. A few questions must be answered. How long should it take from the last period bell to get to the locker room? How long does it take the student to get dressed? How long does it take to get from the locker room to the physical education class activity area? Where will the roll be called?

Elapsed time between classes

An instructor who has been in a school system for a few years might guess as to what constitutes a reasonable length of time. Guessing usually does not make for accuracy. If the instructor is new to the system, he has no basis for a guess. It would seem that the best way for the instructor to find out if the time allowed the student between the last bell and ROLL CALL is fair, would be to travel the same distance himself, noting corridor traffic impediments, dressing time, and how long it would take to make the trip under approximately the same circumstances as the student.

Reasons for tardiness

An allowance must be made for a student being tardy at ROLL CALL for some of the following reasons:

1. The teacher in his last class may have kept the entire group overtime. If this is frequent, then a tactful removal of the cause must be effected, and it might not be easy. Contact the teacher involved in the case.

2. Practical jokers may have hidden vital parts of his clothing, and he hesitates to come forward half dressed.

3. The student had to stop at the restroom.

5

4.   He forgot his locker key .. the combination on the lock would not work .. his pants ripped .. he left his shoes at home .. he slipped on the floor and fell hard.

5.   He has a pain in the neck, and is too sick to work out.

6.   He is just plain slow.

Excused illness

A comment on the person who claims that he is sick and not able to take part in physical education may be in order at this time. There is no way for one person to tell how another feels, so there should be a definite procedure to handle those who are well enough to come to school but not well enough to participate in the physical education classes.

No one would require a sick person to work, but it is relatively easy to determine if there is fever, if he looks sick, if there is inflammation, or if he has an obvious surface injury. In the absence of immediate signs of incapacity, the person should be sent to the school nurse or get clearance through the family physician. A note from home many times covers up for the student. The delicate area of allowable excuses should be studied in planning the program policy. Excuse procedures should be clear to the students. After home confining illness, there should always be medical clearance.

Brevity in conducting the ROLL CALL is most desirable in order to allow more time for conducting regular class matters. The human touch must be retained. As the instructor "walks the line" as described in the next part, the instructor should make a practice of mentally noting the names of the class members. It is important for the individual to have the instructor call him by his name, rather than be addressed as, "You, you stand here," etc.

The mechanics of the <u>ROLL</u> <u>CALL</u>

There are dozens of ways of calling the roll to determine if all who are supposed to be present are in attendance, or to discover some transfers which have not been indicated on the official class roster.

The following are some of the methods in use:

1. Get silence, if possible. The first day you might need a gun, and the second day a whistle, and, after that if all goes well, just hold up the left hand, and with the right hand point to the designated place. Then, call the name of each student and listen carefully for a reply. This method is very time consuming, and the reply may be a pal covering up for a pal, instead of the real thing.

2. Place numbers on the floor and on signal each student stands at his appointed place. Empty numbers are indicated as an absence in the roll books.

3. The authors suggest lining up the students by classes and in alphabetical order. Instructing a few student leaders a little ahead of time is a good way to get the group moving. When the class is in formation, space them approximately one foot apart and require the best possible posture. Starting with the first person, every fifth class member steps forward two paces and accounts for his squad of five. If all are present, he reports "all present." If one is absent, he tells who is absent, and, if possible, the reason as follows: "Joe is not in school today. Pat is visiting with the principal, and told me he would be ten minutes late." If the squad leader is absent, the next one to him takes over.

    Assuming that there are thirty in the class and all are present, it is possible to account for attendance with six "all presents," and in about ten seconds. This way of calling the roll places some desirable responsibility upon the squad captain, and at the same time gives him a little recognition that he might not otherwise receive. The lineup would look something like this:

    C x x x x C x x x x C x x x x C x x x x C x x x x C x x x x

During the actual calling of the roll all C's would step forward one step, one after another and look something like this:

```
x x x x    x x x x    x x x x    x x x x    x x x x    x x x x

C          C          C          C          C          C
```

4.   If the instructor has a method of his own that, due to conditions, is as fast and effective, then by all means it should be used. Since the roll would on occasion be called inside or outside, variations to meet conditions would certainly be in order.

The instructor would do well to frequently "walk the line" while the group is in ROLL CALL formation and have an inspection. The following are things for which to look:

1. Cleanliness of clothes
2. Shoes laced to the top
3. Posture
4. Skin blemishes
5. Personal cleanliness
6. Cuts or bruises
7. Attitude
8. Discharging nose
9. Tilting head
10. Coughing and sneezing
11. Odor
12. Vague expression
13. Scratching
14. Unnatural voice

The instructor must decide whether or not all the students are physically fit to participate in the class. If he notices any who are not fit, he should send them to other quarters for their own well-being and that of the others.

2. ACTIVITY PREPARATION

The most common name for this is "warmup." The phrase suggests heat, getting the body warm. This could be done by any number of exercises requiring more than average effort, or by sitting on a hot radiator. While a good workout to induce perspiration might be desirable, it would seldom be an end in itself. The preparation for the activity of the day should not be just a "warmup," but a series of movements orientated to prepare the student for the stresses to which he will soon be subjected. The following commentary on basic physiological concepts as related to sport skills is the purpose of this part of the CLASS GUIDE FOR PHYSICAL EDUCATION.

Exercises Involving Excessive Muscle Stretching

Are deep-knee bends deleterious to one engaging in strenuous exercises? Perhaps controlled studies would provide the answer, but little has been done in this area. A query on this matter sent to three outstanding physicians, noted for their leadership in the sports medicine field, revealed that two thought deep-knee bends were not harmful, and the third thought they were, if "bounced" in the down position.

Many exercises thought to be harmful have been performed with no pre-conditioning. In reference to deep-knee bends one has to wonder how the Russian dancers continue to move in this fashion, as a normal pursuit, without apparent injury.

One may hear or read comments condemning the duck-waddle exercise, but perhaps these comments stemmed from isolated cases where injury occurred due to lack of pre-conditioning or pre-stretching the muscles over a period of time. Baseball catchers spending many hours over a season's play in similar position to the duck-waddle apparently survive with little damage or injury.

When a body part is forced through an extreme range of motion without pre-conditioning or pre-stretching, damage is almost certain to occur.

Hence, the teacher or coach who contemplates an exercise program for his students should not demand full-range motion immediately, but should over a period of time move slowly toward this objective.

Exercises Defined as to Purpose

Much has been written concerning so-called "warm-up exercises," preceding some activity. Part of the discussion lies, no doubt, in confused opinions as to what is meant by "warm-up exercises," as compared with "stretching exercises," and "conditioning exercises."

One might define warm-up exercises as those involving body movement passing through low ranges and without regard to duration or intensity. In this sense, such warm-up exercises may be totally useless when given to a group with the idea of preventing muscle injury or improving performance.

Warm-up exercises might be defined a bit differently by the coach who is interested in getting a distance runner or a swimmer ready for an event involving cardio-respiratory function approaching the "steady state." In this sense a runner might run five one mile races at a fast pace just prior to the main event. A swimmer may be asked to swim strenuously, for a full hour or more preceding a dual meet. Such an approach to warm-up exercises involves a regular but tolerable degree of body motion; not fully 100 per cent in intensity, but of rather long duration. Performance will be improved when reliance is placed on the steady state, or, in other words, when the body is ready to operate at its physiological best.

Activities not requiring extreme stretching movements can well dispense with warm-up exercises if the objective is to prevent muscle injury.

Stretching exercises, defined as those body movements passing through an extreme range of motion, must be performed slowly with gradually increased range to the maximum point prior to a main effort. If such is not done, injury to muscle tissue is almost certain to occur. Such activities would involve deep knee bends, duck-waddling, leg splits, hurdling, and free exercise.

Conditioning exercises may be defined as those exercises designed to improve the ability of the body to perform at an increased rate of efficiency. Depending on how the exercises are conducted, they may result in improved cardio-respiratory improvement, improved muscular endurance, and/or improved muscular strength.

Cardio-respiratory improvement is inherent in vigorous exercises designed for strength and in those designed for muscular endurance. Muscle strength is gained through progressive resistance exercise. Weight training is a good way to achieve strength in the shortest possible time, but such training does little for improving the cardio-respiratory function. Strength can also be achieved through general calisthenics exercise if the principles of progressive resistance are adhered to.

General Conditioning Exercises Designed for Strength

General conditioning exercises as defined here refer to the series of calisthenic exercises usually administered prior to a class activity. These exercises may be made with the objective of muscular strength in mind. One may start out with ten to twelve exercises to be given to the group. Because of the nature of each exercise, not all will have the same number of repetitions nor the same cadence. However, if strength is an objective, the number of repetitions for each must be increased while the time needed to execute the exercise remains stable or is reduced. This constitutes progressive resistance. The same occurs, however, if the time for each exercise is held constant, but the subject is asked to increase the number of repetitions.

When an instructor uses a set of calisthenics exercises prior to a class period every day for many weeks without paying any attention to the load and time factor, the students are not really getting much out of the exercise except a sort of general "loosening up" workout. Such a method of exercising does have value in stepping up the circulation and in maintaining a level of conditioning already established, but it can hardly be thought of as "improved" conditioning.

General Conditioning Exercises Designed for Muscular Endurance

The value of muscle endurance as compared to the value of muscle strength does not seem to get the specific attention it deserves when one considers various activities. One way to illustrate the difference is to compare the two factors in relation to running. A cross-country runner who will run three miles or more when in training needs a greater reserve of muscle endurance. In contrast, a 100 yard dash man needs some muscular endurance, but relatively speaking he needs a greater amount of muscle strength.

Some skill and sport activities call for strength for short durations of time, while other activities call for the muscles to perform work over a long period of time.

General Conditioning Exercises for Class Work

In regular class work if the objectives are clearly perceived, it may be that the instructor is not interested in improving cardiorespiratory function, muscle strength, or muscle endurance. He may be interested in maintaining the level of muscle tonus at its established peak. In such instances these objectives should be clearly understood and so stated, and should not be considered as achieving the objectives of improved muscle strength or endurance to any great magnitude.

Isometric and Isotonic Exercises Involving Muscle Tissue

The prefix "iso" refers to equality or "sameness." The suffix "metric" refers to measure, and the suffix "tonic" refers to tension. An isometric muscle act refers to the keeping of muscle tissue at the same length (tension) while undergoing stimulation. An attempt to reach down from a standing position to bring an immovable weight to the chest by flexing the lower arms is an example of isometric muscle action. The flexor muscles undergo stimulation and attempt to shorten themselves but are prevented from doing so because of the immovable weight.

Isometric Exercise

At a professional meeting in 1954, Dr. Arthur H Steinhaus[1] restated the results of a study done by Hettinger and Muller in Germany in 1954. Three of the more pertinent findings were as follows:

1. Muscle strength increases an average of 5% per week when the training load is as little as 1/3, or even less, of maximal strength.

2. Muscle strength increases more rapidly with increasing intensity of training load up to about 2/3 of maximal strength. Beyond this, increase in training load has no further effect.

---

[1]Steinhaus, Arthur H, "Some Selected Facts from Physiology to Illustrate Scientific Principles in Athletic Training." C.P.E.A. Proceedings, Fifty-Seventh Annual Meeting. New York City, 1954.

3.   One practice period per day in which the tension was held for six seconds resulted in as much increase in strength as longer periods (up to full exhaustion in 45 seconds) and more frequent practices (up to 7 per day.)

Isotonic Exercise

In an isotonic muscular act, the muscle retains its tension and if capable of doing so, will shorten to its maximum. In the example given above, if the flexor muscles are capable of lifting a lighter weight and it is brought to the chest, then it is an isotonic muscle act.

The use of isotonic exercise for increasing muscle strength could best be brought about by use of variable weights whereby the weights would be carried through a full range of motion for various muscle groups. Such exercises would require some equipment and pre-class arrangement of the equipment.

Perhaps a better plan for increasing muscle strength through isotonic exercise, without need for equipment, would be to use calisthenic exercises as noted earlier. One would simply keep the repetitions constant and reduce the time allotted for completion of a set number, or, one would keep the time constant for each exercise, but increase the number of repetitions.

In the CLASS GUIDES which follow, it would seem best to employ the basic mechanical concepts as related to the activities of the day. The individual needs should determine the assigning or the avoiding of certain activities.

3. RELATED ACTIVITY COMMENTARY

Something specific and related to the student's needs and physical welfare should be taught every class period. Since this will usually follow the ACTIVITY PREPARATION it could be considered a rest period. It would be good procedure to have the students sit on the floor in the same order as they were in for the ROLL CALL. This would be convenient and save time in the event that the instructor wanted to divide his group by counting off. The instructor would also be centered and get maximum attention since his class would be at ease.

The talk might include the rules of the game to be played during the activity to follow, the cautions to be observed in the game, and the techniques and accepted courtesies of the play. If the activity to be pursued were a familiar one, then, possibly the explanation would not be necessary. The games that are to be played in class should be preceded by some drill which would give basic training in the skills involved. The game participants will enjoy the contests most when they have enough skill for at least occasional success.

Nevertheless, something concrete should be taught in every class period, be it a history class, an accounting class, or physical education situation. It is the thought of the authors that a maximum of five minutes should be spent at this time, and probably the ideal would be three minutes, otherwise the other four parts of the period will have to be shortened.

The discussion subject matter might include, in addition to the day's activities: How to cut toenails .. conduct in the locker room .. or even activities outside of the school, such as hunting and camping situations. Included in this text are many outlines of subjects from which the instructor may find items of interest. These topics will suggest many others. Again a caution. The group is probably ready for the ACTIVITY. This time is a breather. Do not make it a preaching situation. Aim at three minutes. It might be wise to use a watch.

4. THE ACTIVITY

The activities will vary with the section of the country, the season, and the interests and needs of the students. A testing program and proper followup would seem to be indicated in about any situation. Records should be kept and improvement noted. It is good motivation to place these records in a prominent place. To avoid embarrassment it is sometimes wise to have a cutoff point. Post only the top half. Little is gained by drawing attention to the poor scores, and unnecessary embarrassment in any situation, social or educational, is not good.

The program should be diversified as much as possible. Use all available facilities. Something is sadly absent from a physical education program that has tennis courts, but no time is used to acquaint the student with the game, gymnastic apparatus that is un-used, tumbling mats, but no instructional unit in that area, and indifference to the interests of the students and the community. The section of the country where water skiing, swimming, fishing, and even sun bathing are possible, should have time devoted to them. In another part of the country the activities may be LaCrosse, Hockey, and Mountain Climbing. A good physical education program must be flexible to meet the needs of the student where he lives.

The students who are not in the varsity athletic activities are being shortchanged when a few games such as basketball inside and softball outside day after day become the physical education program. Unfortunately, even in these games, there may be no instruction, and the student learns by trial and error. Physical education has too much to offer to become merely a situation to store children a few hours a week.

It is not the purpose of physical education, either, to become a farm system for the varsity sports program. This is not intended to imply that the varsity activities be excluded. A good program will acquaint the student with many game and recreational activities, including the games popular in the area. By using faculty assistants, or even student helpers under supervision, it may be desirable and possible to have more than one activity going on at the same time. Facilities, weather, helpers, materials, and the immediate situation will determine the best outline to follow. An occasional movie of the Olympics, the World Series, or the showing of the many audiovisual aids available to demonstrate skills, is a good change of pace, presents a good learning situation, and may create in the student a desire to excel.

Planning the class by season makes a logical program arrangement for many parts of the country. The following is an example:

Fall: September to October 31

Medical Examinations	Touch Football
Tennis	Cross Country
Strength and Agility Tests	Obstacle Courses
Volleyball	Kittenball
Soccer	Game Ability Tests
Hiking	Speedball

Early Winter: November 1 to December 23

Basketball Fundamentals	Shuffleboard
Tumbling	Apparatus Work
Bowling	Swimming
Close Order Drills	Square Dancing
Corkball	Weight Lifting

Late Winter: January 2 to March 15

Relays	Intramurals
Badminton	Area Winter Sports
Handball	Squash
Hockey	Wrestling
Rope Work	Individual Preferences
Table Tennis	Lifesaving

Spring: March 15 to June

Tennis	Track and Field Events
Golf	Group Games
Mass Activities	Low Organization Games
Softball	Archery
Horse Shoes	Re-testing
Fishing Implements	Rowing

5. DISMISSAL

The dismissal should be timed to allow the student to shower, to dress, and to get to his next class on time. The instructor might time himself in this activity. The reverse of the situation is present here, when compared to the ROLL CALL. If the student is late for his next class, the instructor may expect a friendly (?) visit from the teacher who is having his students arrive late as a result of delayed physical education class dismissal. Again, the slow student may enter the picture. He may be slow because of his fault, or possibly because of others.

The instructor or someone in a position to give adequate supervision should be in the dressing room. The shower should be more than a rinse, and a towel should be used. Underwear placed on a wet body makes an undesirable blotter. The presence of an instructor helps to maintain order and minimize roughhouse activity. Few things in a dressing room are soft. Floors tend to be slippery, and a fall may result in a serious injury. This is a good time to check for injuries that have not been reported. Discourage the unsanitary practice of trading or borrowing of clothing.

Someone has to keep locker room discipline, turn off the lights, close the windows, shut off the showers, report clogged sewers, and to be sure that towels, soap, and school property are handled according to a plan. The procedure should be set up at the start of each school year.

The physical education class is over when the last boy leaves the area. Good housekeeping on the part of the students will raise your ranking with the maintenance men. Their opinions may be highly respected in the community.

CHAPTER   II.

C L A S S   G U I D E S

F O R   T H E

V A R I O U S   S E A S O N S

1.   Fall

2.   Early Winter

3.   Late Winter

4.   Spring

****

The Conduct of Physical Education Classes

1. The daily period in physical education should not be less than forty minutes. Sixty minutes works out best, because that allows more time for dressing and the shower.

2. The program must be modified for pupils whose physical or emotional condition prevent their full participation.

3. A health examination should be required of all pupils each year or oftener if the student appears to have need for it.

4. Cumulative records of the health examinations should be kept on hand and be easily available.

5. Cumulative records of tests and skill performances should also be kept. Comparisons of these records help measure a students progress and can also be used for motivation.

6. Let the students and parents and the faculty know the objectives of the course.

7. Do not hesitate to vary the program to meet the needs of the students and the community.

8. Make it a point at each class meeting to add something to the students knowledge of health and recreations. Three minutes a day spent in this field can often make a lasting impression on students.

9. The class should be dressed in appropriate costumes, and generally it is best if all are dressed the same.

10. The instructor should be dressed in gym clothes and look like a physical education instructor.

11. Students should be expected to take a shower after each class.

12. Explanation, demonstration, and participation is good physical education teaching technique.

13. Constantly emphasize character training and sportsmanship.

14. Physical education must earn the privilege of enjoying equal status with all parts of the school program.

15. Locker room conduct should not be taken for granted, but supervision must be provided as in the gymnasium. It is necessary that order prevail if accidents are to be prevented.

16. Opportunities for developing leadership and responsibility should be provided by the use of squad captains, particularly in the calling of the roll, conduct of intramurals, and the care of equipment.

17. Arrange that all students have an equal opportunity to excel and that no individual or group consistently controls the parts of the program.

18. The whistle can only mean stop or go. Decide which, and usually it is best to be used for stopping an activity.

19. Arrange to have all necessary equipment on hand before the period starts, and arrange for its orderly return.

20. Don't bore the class. Physical education is a time for activity. Have the activity, promote it, and keep it under control.

No. 1.

FALL

****

September 1 to October 31 . . . Class No. 1

1. ROLL CALL

    a. Street clothes
    b. Divide group into squads of five
    c. C xxxx C xxxx C xxxx C xxxx C xxxx C xxxx
    d. Practice getting into position several times.

2. ACTIVITY PREPARATION

    a. Practice getting into half-circle formation
    b. Practice getting into exercise formation
    c. Practice getting into relay formation.

3. RELATED ACTIVITY COMMENTARY

    a. Practice sitting in semi-circle in ROLL CALL order
    b. Explain that the purpose of the course is to improve
       physical efficiency and to develop good health habits
    c. Give time and place for medical examinations
    d. Tell place of bulletin board for all news relative to class.

4. THE ACTIVITY

    a. Time the group calling the ROLL
    b. Time the group getting into ACTIVITY FORMATION
    c. Time group changing to various formations.

5. DISMISSAL

    a. Lead the class to the locker room
    b. Impress and explain the discipline expected
    c. Dismiss on time for the next class.

Additional Information sources:
Kozman, Hilda, et al., Methods in Physical Education, W.C. Brown Co., Dubuque, Iowa, 1964.
Kilander, H. Frederick, School Health Education, Prentice-Hall, Inc. Englewood Cliffs, New Jersey, 1965.

1. <u>ROLL CALL</u>

2. <u>ACTIVITY PREPARATION</u>

3. <u>RELATED ACTIVITY COMMENTARY</u>

4. <u>THE ACTIVITY</u>

5. <u>DISMISSAL</u>

_____

Additional information sources:

September 1 to October 31 . . . Class No. 2

1. ROLL CALL

    a. Street clothes
    b. Note those present, transferred, and those absent.

2. ACTIVITY PREPARATION

    a. Practice getting into formation
    b. Use student leaders and note natural leaders
    c. Use simple activities as a trial run, some that require
        little effort: right hand up .. left hand up .. both hands up
    d. Hands on hips, balance on left foot fifteen seconds
    e. Hands on hips, balance on right foot fifteen seconds.

3. RELATED ACTIVITY COMMENTARY

    a. Check on medical examinations to see list of those fit
    b. Explain voluntary insurance program
    c. Clarify the method for getting excuses before or after ab-
        sences.

4. THE ACTIVITY

    a. Take group for a tour of the inside of the gymnasium
    b. Explain the purpose of various apparatus and the checkout
        system for materials
    c. Caution about participation on equipment without having
        had adequate instruction.

5. DISMISSAL

    a. Assign lockers.
    b. Explain the way to store clothes so that they will dry in
        the lockers
    c. Dismiss on time and note the time.

Additional information sources:
Webster, Randolph W., Philosophy of Physical Education, W.C.
Brown Co., Dubuque, Iowa, 1965.
Mueller, Pat and Mitchel, Elmer D., Intramural Sports, 3rd edition
The Ronald Press, New York, 1960.

1. ROLL CALL

2. ACTIVITY PREPARATION

3. RELATED ACTIVITY COMMENTARY

4. THE ACTIVITY

5. DISMISSAL

_____

Additional information sources:

September 1 to October 31 ... Class No. 3

1. <u>ROLL</u> <u>CALL</u>

   a. Street clothes
   b. Demand precision and speed
   c. Scuttle any attempts at clowning
   d. Watch latecomers and ascertain the reason.

2. <u>ACTIVITY</u> <u>PREPARATION</u>

   a. Run to various formations
   b. To protect hardwood floors shoes might be removed, but this could invite problems. Slippery floors can cause injury
   c. Comment on conduct expected in class
   d. Medical examinations.

3. <u>RELATED</u> <u>ACTIVITY</u> <u>COMMENTARY</u>

   a. Announce that gym clothes will be required for the next class and where and how to get them
   b. Describe in detail how to dress
   c. Lace shoes to the top
   d. Indicate the need for fresh clean clothing frequently.

4. <u>THE</u> <u>ACTIVITY</u>

   a. Tour the outside area to be used for physical education
   b. Walk around the track
   c. Explain with pride the facilities and how they can help the individual
   d. Caution about travel in the paths of balls, discus, or impeding runners.

5. <u>DISMISSAL</u>

   a. Practice finding lockers
   b. Work out a system to avoid crowding in showers.

Additional information sources:
Barrow, Harold M. and Crisp, Marjorie, et al., <u>Physical</u> <u>Education</u>
<u>Syllabus</u>, Burgess Publishing Company, Minneapolis, Minnesota, 1961.

1. <u>ROLL CALL</u>

2. <u>ACTIVITY   PREPARATION</u>

3. <u>RELATED ACTIVITY COMMENTARY</u>

4. <u>THE ACTIVITY</u>

5. <u>DISMISSAL</u>

Additional information sources:

September 1 to October 31 ... Class No. 4

1. ROLL CALL

    a. Gym clothes for all for the first time
    b. Note time it takes the first and last boy to arrive
    c. See privately those who did not get dressed.

2. ACTIVITY PREPARATION

    a. Line up in exercise formation
    b. Run in position 10 seconds . . do 5 pushups
    c. Repeat until there is evidence of some fatigue
    d. Use a buddy to hold feet and do 5 to 10 situps.

3. RELATED ACTIVITY COMMENTARY

    a. Explain the purpose of previous exercises, and
    b. Those exercises designed to build strength . . endurance . .
       general conditioning.

4. THE ACTIVITY

    Good weather ... outside
    a. 440 yards, walk 50 steps .. run 50 steps .. try for the
       distance in exactly 100 seconds
    b. Repeat the distance, but lower the time .. announce all
       times
    c. Play a circle game .. one or more groups.

5. DISMISSAL

    a. Dismiss a few minutes early
    b. Stay in the shower room .. note injuries
    c. Call attention to the danger of scalding in the shower
    d. Inspect locker arrangement.

Additional information sources:
Seaton, Don Cash, et al., Physical Education Handbook, Prentice-Hall,
Inc., Englewood Cliffs, New Jersey, 1965.
Logan, Gene A. and Dunbleberg, James, Adaptations of Physical
Activity, Wadsworth Publishing Co., Belmont, California, 1964.

1. <u>ROLL CALL</u>

2. <u>ACTIVITY</u> <u>PREPARATION</u>

3. <u>RELATED ACTIVITY COMMENTARY</u>

4. <u>THE</u> <u>ACTIVITY</u>

5. <u>DISMISSAL</u>

_____

Additional information sources:

September 1 to October 31 ... Class No. 5

1. ROLL CALL

    a. Gym clothes should be worn by all
    b. Give misfits an opportunity to be fitted
    c. Verify medical examinations.

2. ACTIVITY PREPARATION

    a. Arrange, privately, activities for the partially handicapped
    b. Be sure that permanently excused students are assigned to a place where they can be accounted for.

3. RELATED ACTIVITY COMMENTARY

    a. Encourage boys to indicate their special interest areas .. archery .. varsity ambitions ..
    b. Note those with leadership qualities
    c. Call attention to the library information sources in areas of individual interest.

4. THE ACTIVITY

    a. Walk two or three miles over a definite course
    b. Occasionally jog 100 steps and walk 50. Note laggers and those eager to cover the distance quickly
    c. End the period with a simple circle game.

5. DISMISSAL

    a. Control profanity on first offense
    b. Keep close watch on sox and be sure that they are changed often
    c. Encourage proper body drying, particularly between the toes.

Additional information sources:
Wadsworth Publishing Company, Inc., Belmont, California, has available at a nominal fee a series with such titles as Beginning Tennis, Beginning Volleyball, Beginning Badminton, etc.
Kilander, H. Frederick, Health for Modern Living, 2nd edition, Prentice-Hall, Inc., Englewood Cliffs, New Jersey, 1965.

1. <u>ROLL CALL</u>

2. <u>ACTIVITY PREPARATION</u>

3. <u>RELATED ACTIVITY COMMENTARY</u>

4. <u>THE ACTIVITY</u>

5. <u>DISMISSAL</u>

Additional information sources:

September 1 to October 31

1. ROLL CALL

    a. Check footwear for proper type and lacing
    b. Note if all are wearing a supporter
    c. Insist on the wearing of a T shirt. Some schools frown on upper trunk nudity.

2. ACTIVITY PREPARATION

    a. Seven minutes of general conditioning exercises
    b. Place emphasis on stretching.

3. RELATED ACTIVITY COMMENTARY

    History of tennis .. explain unusual method of scoring .. 5 - 30 - 40 - Game, instead of 1 - 2 - 3 - 4. Singles court the same as doubles, except narrower. With diagram show where the server first hits the ball to start play. Avoid detailed explanation of grips and strategy.

4. THE ACTIVITY

    Tennis is best taught with the whole method. Just have the boys start playing to get the idea of scoring and the general plan of play. Have a student assistant bring school rackets and balls to the court. Try to get in at least three or four sessions for each boy, and, if possible, keep sessions close together. Encourage play outside of school.

    16-inch softball for other part of class. End softball play with 880 jog, but note time of front runners.

5. DISMISSAL

    a. Is the hot water hot? Be sure the water is turned off.

_____

Additional information sources:
Hillas, Marjorie and LeFevre, John R., Tennis, a Manual for Teachers with Materials, Methods, Programs for Group Instruction, W.C. Brown Co., Dubuque, Iowa, 1955.

1. ROLL   CALL

2. ACTIVITY   PREPARATION

3. RELATED ACTIVITY COMMENTARY

4. THE   ACTIVITY

5. DISMISSAL

────────────

Additional information sources:

September 1 to October 31

1.   ROLL CALL

   a. No Lineup. Note absences while program is in progress.

2.   ACTIVITY PREPARATION

   a. Nearby college gymnastic team is presenting a demonstration involving activities possible for some members of your classes *
   b. Check out public address system ahead of time, because an explanation of the routines adds much to the interest.

3.   RELATED ACTIVITY COMMENTARY

   a. Introduce the instructor in charge of the performing guests and let him take over.

4.   THE ACTIVITY

   a. The guests provide the activity
   b. Courtesy would require good attention and properly timed applause
   c. Thank the performing group at the conclusion
   d. Give recognition to any who might have been former students of the school
   e. Allow time for your class to meet the performers and ask questions.

5.   DISMISSAL

   a. Dismiss as any other academic class
   b. Be sure that the class leaves orderly
   c. Refreshments and a simple reception might be in order.

----

*Contact the colleges with physical education teacher training departments. Most of them have groups available for exhibitions at little or no charge. They are usually eager to give the incentive of performance and applause to their groups.

1. <u>ROLL CALL</u>

2. <u>ACTIVITY PREPARATION</u>

3. <u>RELATED ACTIVITY COMMENTARY</u>

4. <u>THE ACTIVITY</u>

5. <u>DISMISSAL</u>

Additional information sources:

September 1 to October 31

1. ROLL CALL

    a. Urge use of warm clothing on cool days when outside
    b. Make managers of those who evidence interest in physical activity, but for physical reasons may not be permitted to participate.

2. ACTIVITY PREPARATION

    a. Once around the track .. 440 yards .. no timing
    b. 10 bell rockers
    c. 10 squat thrusts
    d. Give an opportunity for class members to stand on head 10 seconds for A. A. A. Be sure to teach roll out when over balanced.

3. RELATED ACTIVITY COMMENTARY

    Explain football .. dangers inherent in unprotected sandlot play .. give specific don'ts for flag football, .. accidental tackling, clipping, and piling on.

4. THE ACTIVITY

    a. Flag football
    b. Horseshoes or shuffleboard for those needing less vigorous activity
    c. Losers of games jog around the track once just before dismissal.

5. DISMISSAL

    a. Watch for shoulder scratches
    b. Clean grass burns and any other abrasions
    c. Call attention of maintenance men to any plumbing deficiencies in the shower room.

Additional information sources:
Griffin, J.H., Handbook for Student Athletic Managers, School Aid Company, Danville, Illinois, 1964.

1. ROLL CALL

2. ACTIVITY PREPARATION

3. RELATED ACTIVITY COMMENTARY

4. THE ACTIVITY

5. DISMISSAL

_____

Additional information sources:

September 1 to October 31

1. ROLL CALL

   a. Gym clothes for all
   b. Be prepared to handle those who hesitate to disrobe in front of others.

2. ACTIVITY PREPARATION

   a. Run in position .. 10 seconds, rest 10 and repeat
   b. 6 situps with the help of a buddy, then reverse
   c. 10 squat thrusts
   d. 15 jumping jacks.

3. RELATED ACTIVITY COMMENTARY

   a. Explain desirable weight at various ages. Point out current fallacies.
   b. Encourage boys to participate in non-varsity activities such as archery, tumbling, or areas that meet their special interests.

4. THE ACTIVITY

   The plan to go outside has been cancelled because of bad weather.
   a. Practice counting off by 4's, 5's, and other numbers. Try for military precision
   b. Form relay teams
      1. Run to the opposite wall and return
      2. Run to the opposite wall with partner
      3. Run to the opposite wall, hands and feet, belly up. Repeat head leading, then feet leading.

5. DISMISSAL

   a. Watch for shower skippers.

Additional information sources:
Downer, Robert J., et al., Exploring Physical Education, Wadsworth Publishing Co., Belmont, California, 1965.

1. ROLL CALL

2. ACTIVITY PREPARATION

3. RELATED ACTIVITY COMMENTARY

4. THE ACTIVITY

5. DISMISSAL

Additional information sources:

September 1 to October 31

1. <u>ROLL CALL</u>

   a. Practice counting off
   b. Run to opposite side and call the roll.

2. <u>ACTIVITY PREPARATION</u>

   a. Five exercises designed to develop muscular strength.
      (See chapters dealing with exercise as to purpose.)

3. <u>RELATED ACTIVITY COMMENTARY</u>

   a. Keep gym clothing and towels clean
   b. All personal clothing should be identified by number
      or name. The equipment managers have <u>free</u> indelible
      ink.

4. <u>THE ACTIVITY</u>

   a. Keep tennis courts occupied with beginners. Use
      student varsity assistants. Check with tennis coach.
      Aim is to acquaint the entire class with the game
   b. ALL AROUND ATHLETE 880 yard test in 2:45 or
      less qualifies. Announce all times at the finish line
   c. Be sure there is adequate preparation before this activity
   d. A. A. A. 100 yards in 12 seconds or less. Give in-
      struction in starting.

5. <u>DISMISSAL</u>

   a. Dismiss on time, regardless of enthusiasm
   b. Caution about distracting noises when passing open
      classroom windows
   c. Dry with a towel thoroughly.

Additional information sources:
Robinson, Al., <u>Physical Education Class Record Book</u>, School Aid
Company, Danville, Illinois.
Dolan, Joseph P., <u>Treatment and Prevention of Athletic Injuries</u>,
Interstate Printers and Publishers, Inc., Danville, Illinois, 1967

1. <u>ROLL CALL</u>

2. <u>ACTIVITY PREPARATION</u>

3. <u>RELATED ACTIVITY COMMENTARY</u>

4. <u>THE ACTIVITY</u>

5. <u>DISMISSAL</u>

———————————

Additional information sources:

September 1 to October 31

1. ROLL CALL

    a. Compliment prompt attendance
    b. Practice counting off in military fashion.

2. ACTIVITY PREPARATION

    a. 10 straddle jumps
    b. 25 pushups .. for A. A. A. point
    c. 10 body extensions .. heels off floor .. hold extension
        5 seconds
    d. 10 squat thrusts
    e. Run in position 30 seconds, rest and repeat.

3. RELATED ACTIVITY COMMENTARY

    a. Explain the ALL AROUND ATHLETE plan .. its benefits
        . . and rewards
    b. See section of this GUIDE for the A. A. A. activities and
        standards. Also, the A. A. A. A. A. for those less mature.

4. THE ACTIVITY

    Inside or outside .. A. A. A. trials
    a. Jump over the foot
    b. 25 bellystretchers
    c. Stand on head 10 seconds. Be sure the tuck and roll out from
        losing balance has been taught
    d. Run the mile .. 6 minutes or less qualifies. Note and care
        for exhaustion.

5. DISMISSAL

    a. Note complaints of excessive fatigue
    b. Watch for athletes foot or irritation in crotch area. Faulty
        drying or ill-fitting trunks may be the cause.

Additional information sources:
Griffin, J.H., "All Around Athletic Tests and Standards," Scholastic
Coach, 24:54-55, November, 1954.

1. ROLL CALL

2. ACTIVITY PREPARATION

3. RELATED ACTIVITY COMMENTARY

4. THE ACTIVITY

5. DISMISSAL

_____

Additional information sources:

No. 2.

EARLY WINTER

****

November 1 to December 23

1. ROLL CALL

    a. Watch for signs of flu and other respiratory ailments.

2. ACTIVITY PREPARATION

    a. Five muscular endurance exercises .. six minutes.

3. RELATED ACTIVITY COMMENTARY

Short history of basketball .. started at Springfield (Mass.) College in 1891 by Dr. James Naismith .. invented to keep boys busy after the football season .. peach baskets were nailed to a track balcony that circled gym .. balcony was ten feet high, hence the present height. First games played with ten to twelve on a side, but soon the ideal number became five. Basic rules have changed little.

4. THE ACTIVITY

    a. Teach guard around drill at northeast and southeast goals

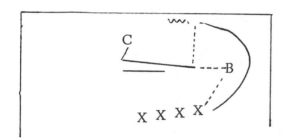

X passes to B. X goes outside of B. B passes to C. C passes to X, who shoots. Drill progresses by B going to back of the line, C takes Bs place, and X takes Cs.

    b. Shuffleboard .. introduce game to six freshmen
    c. Badminton .. introduce game to six. Student assistant
    d. After ten minutes of "a" have half floor scrimmage to demonstrate use of guard around maneuver.

5. DISMISSAL

    a. Dry completely to guard against colds.

Additional information sources:
Pinholster, G.F., Encyclopedia of Basketball Drills, Prentice-Hall, Inc., Englewood Cliffs, New Jersey,

1. ROLL CALL

2. ACTIVITY PREPARATION

3. RELATED ACTIVITY COMMENTARY

4. THE ACTIVITY

5. DISMISSAL

———————————

Additional information sources:

November 1 to December 23

1. ROLL CALL

    a. Stand at attention, toes exactly on the line
    b. A good snappy roll call starts the class off right.

2. ACTIVITY PREPARATION

    a. Five muscular endurance exercises
    b. Give opportunity to get A. A. A. point with bellystretchers
        Count off by 2's. First the ONES try for 25 stretches with
        the 2's counting, and then reverse the order of trial.

3. RELATED ACTIVITY COMMENTARY

    Explain how tourney mathematics work. The series of 2 - 4 -
    8 - 16, etc. There are always the same number of byes as the
    difference between the number entered in a tourney and the next
    perfect multiple of four. For example: 17 in a tourney. The
    next perfect multiple is 32. 17 from 32 would mean 15 byes.
    There are always the same number of contests in a tourney as
    the number of teams entered, minus one. Third place adds one
    more contest.

4. THE ACTIVITY

    Relays to teach the dribble in basketball.
    Divide into four or five groups,
    a. Dribble to the end of the gym and back
    b. Dribble to the end of the gym, but do a complete turn mid-
        way in the run
    c. Dribble to the end of the gym, one half with the right hand,
        and one half with the left hand
    d. Dribble to end of gym making a complete turn at the one-
        third mark and the two-thirds mark.

5. DISMISSAL

    a. Watch for signs of soreness between toes.

Additional Information sources:
Means, Louis E., Intramurals, Their Organization and Administration,
Prentice-Hall, Englewood Cliffs, N.J., 1963.

1. ROLL CALL

2. ACTIVITY PREPARATION

3. RELATED ACTIVITY COMMENTARY

4. THE ACTIVITY

5. DISMISSAL

Additional information sources:

November 1 to December 23

1. ROLL CALL

    a. Let all No. 2 squad men call the roll
    b. Follow up on frequent absentees with the principal.

2. ACTIVITY PREPARATION

    a. Jog around the gym .. high steps .. goose steps, etc.
    b. Allow the students a few minutes for free stretching
       exercises .. suggest a few.

3. RELATED ACTIVITY COMMENTARY

    Explain the purpose of sport ability tests. Indicate how they
    tend to show probable success in competitive varsity sports,
    such as baseball, football, and basketball. Also, point out
    their limitations: Endurance, the ability to adjust to adverse
    circumstances, etc. The basketball test usually takes at
    least two periods. Test helpers should be thoroughly briefed.

4. THE ACTIVITY

    a. Hit the wall from 8 feet, 15 seconds, any type of throw
    b. Hit the torso of a man at 15 feet, two hand pass
    c. Jump and reach. Mark wall standing, and then try to ex-
       ceed the mark by jumping as high as possible
    d. 10 layup shots dribbling around a chair at the free throw line
    e. 20 shots. 5 at free throw line, 5 at far left of line, 5 at
       far right of line, and 5 at the top of the circle
       Activities may be done in any order.

5. DISMISSAL

    a. Note complaints of petty thievery
    b. The presence of a monitor discourages locker looting.

The above test was devised in part by Dr. Brace of Iowa about 1930.
Griffin, J.H., "A Critical Study of a Basketball Motor Ability Test as
Conducted at Teutopolis Community High School from 1933 through
1953." Unpublished.

1. ROLL CALL

2. ACTIVITY PREPARATION

3. RELATED ACTIVITY COMMENTARY

4. THE ACTIVITY

5. DISMISSAL

———————

Additional information sources:

PERSONNEL ASSIGNMENTS FOR ADMINISTERING THE BASKETBALL TEST

1. Hit the Wall 15 seconds at 8 feet   _____

   a. Clerk should have the roster on a clipboard
   b. Stopwatch. Punch the watch when the ball first hits the wall
   c. Count the hits aloud
   d. Give complete instructions to each one being tested. The ball may be thrown in any manner. Do not cross the line. Missed balls must be retrieved with the watch running. One point for each strike.

2. Hit the torso of a man at 15 feet. Two hand push pass
   a. Clipboard with the roster   _____
   b. Watch stepping over the line and do not count those hits
   c. Hitting outline of torso is a good throw
   d. Two points for each hit

3. Jump and Reach
   a. Clipboard and roster
   b. Extra chalk and a yardstick   _____
   c. Be sure contestant extends full length for the first mark
   d. Three tries. Take best try. One point for each inch
   e. Call attention of maintenance men to wall before and after test

4. Dribble Around Chair For Layup

   a. Clipboard with roster   _____
   b. Sit on the chair that is object of drill
   c. Be sure that the dribble is legal
   d. Illegal dribble would invalidate a successful shot
   e. 10 tries. Two points for each try

5. 20 shots at 4 positions
   a. Clipboard and roster
   b. Mark spots on the floor clearly with chalk   _____
   c. At least one foot should be on the mark while shooting
   d. No running shot
   e. Shoot 5 at free throw line, 5 at left edge of free throw line, 5 at right edge of free throw line, 5 at top of free throw circle,

Chief clerk gathers tally sheets, does the necessary calculations, and then gives the results to the instructor. Post top half of those tested.

<u>NOTES:</u>

November 1 to December 23

1. <u>ROLL</u> <u>CALL</u> .. street clothes

    Call the roll in the usual manner.

2. <u>ACTIVITY</u> <u>PREPARATION</u>

    None.

3. <u>RELATED</u> <u>ACTIVITY</u> <u>COMMENTARY</u>

    It is natural for everyone to want to excel in something. By this time, particularly, among freshmen the facilities for physical education should be known. Now is the time to find out those activities which are available that have special appeal, and to whom.

    Three elements are necessary: The facilities. The instructional staff. The desire and ability of the prospective performers.

    The following are some activities that are not common over the nation. But, if any are in your locality, then interest to build special skills in them should be developed:

Swimming	..	Needed a pool	Competent instruction
Fencing	..	Mat .. weapons	" "
Skiing	..	Snow .. terrain	" "
Wrestling	..	Mats and space	" "
Squash	..	Rackets and court	" "
Riding	..	Horses and area	" "

    Survey your situation and add to the list local activities with high interest.

4. <u>THE</u> <u>ACTIVITY</u> .. none.

5. <u>DISMISSAL</u> .. on time.

57

1. <u>ROLL</u> <u>CALL</u>

2. <u>ACTIVITY</u> <u>PREPARATION</u>

3. <u>RELATED</u> <u>ACTIVITY</u> <u>COMMENTARY</u>

4. <u>THE</u> <u>ACTIVITY</u>

5. <u>DISMISSAL</u>

―――――――

Additional information sources:

November 1 to December 23

1. ROLL CALL

    a. Note temperature in gym. If it is too hot, call this to the attention of the maintenance men. They should set thermostats.

2. ACTIVITY PREPARATION

    a. Give four strength building exercises
    b. A. A. A. point for 25 pushups
        Count off by 2's. First the ONES try for 25, then reverse the order of trial. Watch for proper form.

3. RELATED ACTIVITY COMMENTARY

    Explain how league play mathematics work. Use a chalkboard. N (N - 1) over 2 is the number of contests in one round robin. Hence, with 7 teams playing each other once, it would work out as follows: 7 x 6 equals 42. 42 divided by 2 equals 21 contests. Caution: Do not use too much time, because the ACTIVITY is what the class wants.

4. THE ACTIVITY

    a. Fun relays involving a basketball. Divide into groups with an even number
        1. Dribble to end of gym and back, hold hand of partner. One dribbles the up trip, and then reverse
        2. Dribble to end of gym and back riding piggyback. One is the rider on the way up, and then reverse on the way back
        3. Dribble to end of court and back. Two boys carry one dribbling. Change riders
        4. Half floor scrimmage for the remaining time.

5. DISMISSAL

    Check on the use of soap

Additional information sources:
Means, Louis E., and Jack, Harold K., <u>Physical Education Activities, Sports, and Games</u>, Wm. C. Brown Co., Dubuque, Iowa, 1965.

1. ROLL CALL

2. ACTIVITY PREPARATION

3. RELATED ACTIVITY COMMENTARY

4. THE ACTIVITY

5. DISMISSAL

———————

Additional information sources:

November 1 to December 23

1. ROLL CALL

    Practice counting off by 2s .. 4s .. 5s .. etc.

2. ACTIVITY PREPARATION

    a. Present five isometric exercises. Be sure there is adequate explanation and demonstration
    b. Use three men for chinning and alternate boys.

3. RELATED ACTIVITY COMMENTARY

    Explain the hazards inherent with cold weather sports .. thin ice .. frostbite .. hard falls on ice .. tumbling from equipment on snow slopes .. and the recommended first aid, dealing with what to do and what not to do.

4. THE ACTIVITY

    Basketball unit
    a. Layup shot .. be sure the correct leg is raised. Right knee goes up for the right hand, left leg for the left hand shooter. Lightly placing the foot on the shoe of the boy who has a tendency to raise the wrong foot may help him
    b. Give individual instruction off to one side for those having difficulty learning the coordination
    c. Two on one, from about 25 feet out. Alternate the one
    d. Half floor scrimmage from as many stations as possible
    e. Use senior assistants to teach the layup and pivot on correct foot.

5. DISMISSAL

    a. Note knee burns .. if injuries are present, clean thoroughly and lightly bandage
    b. Be alert for sprained ankles.

Additional information sources:
Pinholster, Garland F., Illustrated Basketball Coaching Techniques, Prentice-Hall, Inc., Englewood Cliffs, New Jersey, 1965.

61

1. ROLL CALL

2. ACTIVITY PREPARATION

3. RELATED ACTIVITY COMMENTARY

4. THE ACTIVITY

5. DISMISSAL

_____

Additional information sources:

November 1 to December 23

1. <u>ROLL CALL</u>

    a. Check on student recording the roll
    b. Is the time between the last class and roll call long enough?

2. <u>ACTIVITY PREPARATION</u>

    Do the following exercises in cadence
    a. 30 straddle jumps
    b. 20 pushups
    c. 15 squat thrusts
    d. bellyrockers
    e. Run in position 30 seconds
    f. March smartly around the gym .. square corners .. in
       step .. good posture .. last half modified sprint.

3. <u>RELATED ACTIVITY COMMENTARY</u>

    Keep shoes clean .. inside and out .. powder frequently ..
    lace the entire shoe .. replace laces when knotted .. the shoes
    should be proper for the activity.

4. <u>THE ACTIVITY</u>

    Introduce a tumbling unit
    a. Forward rolls with and without hands
    b. Backward rolls with and without hands
    c. Double roll .. use boys of like size
    d. Thigh stand from a crotch lift .. SPOT
    End all activities with a professional flourish. Those who show
    interest and aptitude should be encouraged to work out for the
    annual physical education demonstration.

5. <u>DISMISSAL</u>

    Look for mat burns

Additional information sources:
Provaznik, Marie and Zabka, Norma B., <u>Gymnastic Activities With</u>
<u>Hand Apparatus for Girls and Boys,</u> Burgess Publishing Co., Minne-
apolis, Minnesota, 1965.

1. ROLL CALL

2. ACTIVITY PREPARATION

3. RELATED ACTIVITY COMMENTARY

4. THE ACTIVITY

5. DISMISSAL

_____

Additional information sources:

November 1 to December 23 - outside

1. ROLL CALL

   a. Urge use of extra clothing for cool days, and cover after strenuous events.
   b. Note and see privately any indications of boils or skin infections.

2. ACTIVITY PREPARATION

   a. Jog around the track, 440 yards, add occasional short sprints.
   b. Stretching exercises .. general conditioning, too.

3. RELATED ACTIVITY COMMENTARY

   a. A. A. A. trials for the broad jump, 17 feet minimum.
   b. A. A. A. trials for 100 yards, 12 seconds minimum.
   c. A. A. A. trials for 440 yards, 60 seconds minimum.
   d. A. A. A. trials for mile, 6 minutes minimum.

4. THE ACTIVITY

   a. When contestants feel that they are ready, allow them to go to their stations as they choose.
   b. The last events, since they are exhausting, should be either the 440 yards or the mile.
   c. Be sure that timers, starters, and tape boys are ready.
   d. Allow sufficient time for 440 and mile boys to recuperate before their next class.

5. DISMISSAL

   a. Have rubdown liniment available. It is not a cure for stiffness and so explain.
   b. Be sure that runners are O. K. before they leave.

Additional information sources:
Doherty, J. Kenneth, Modern Training for Running, Prentice-Hall, Inc., Englewood Cliffs, New Jersey, 1964.
Nixon, John E. and Jewett, Ann E., Physical Education Curriculum, The Ronald Press Co., New York, N. Y., 1964.

1. <u>ROLL CALL</u>

2. <u>ACTIVITY PREPARATION</u>

3. <u>RELATED ACTIVITY COMMENTARY</u>

4. <u>THE ACTIVITY</u>

5. <u>DISMISSAL</u>

_____

Additional information sources:

November 1 to December 23

1. ROLL CALL

    Let all No. 3 squad men take place of the captain in calling the roll.

2. ACTIVITY PREPARATION

    Encourage free choice of activity to loosen up and prepare for completing physical efficiency tests. Allow about 7 minutes.

3. RELATED ACTIVITY COMMENTARY

    Indicate the high scores to date in various events. A test measures certain skills and does not always guarantee success in competition. The ability to keep working without supervision, competitive desire .. these can compensate for a certain amount of skill shortage.

4. THE ACTIVITY

    a. Continue the testing program
    b. Do not allow any distractions to bother those being tested
    c. Be sure that the administration of the test is consistent and that all are working under ideal conditions
    d. Encourage those that are not doing very well.

5. DISMISSAL

    Note speed of those who have been repeatedly late for their next class. See them privately.

Additional information sources:
Cowell, Charles C. and France, William L., Philosophy and Principles of Physical Education, Prentice-Hall, Englewood Cliffs, New Jersey, 1963.
Meyers, Carlton and Blesh, T. Erwin, Measurement in Physical Education, The Ronald Press Co., New York, N.Y., 1962.
Clarke, H. Harrison, Application of Measurement to Health and Physical Education, Prentice-Hall Inc., New York, N.Y., 1959.

1. ROLL CALL

2. ACTIVITY PREPARATION

3. RELATED ACTIVITY COMMENTARY

4. THE ACTIVITY

5. DISMISSAL

_____

Additional information sources:

November 1 to December 23

1. ROLL CALL

Let all No. 3 squad men take place of the captain in calling the roll.

2. ACTIVITY PREPARATION

    a. Circle shoulders
    b. Situps .. with assistance
    c. Trunk twisting, right and left
    d. Pushups
    e. Forward and back trunk bends
    f. Bicycle
    g. A few laps around the gym.

3. RELATED ACTIVITY COMMENTARY

Explain the purpose of so-called warmup exercises .. their need and their limitations. Explain how the tilting plane increases the difficulty of the situp. Comment on the advertisements that indicate they will build muscles and strength.

4. THE ACTIVITY

    a. Striking bag unit starts
    b. Badminton unit continues
    c. Stunts: Stump walk .. various animal walks .. monkey walk Inverted walk on hands and feet .. shoulder stand of light boy on knees and thighs of large under boy .. add as many more as skill and interest indicates.

5. DISMISSAL

Report sluggish drains.

Additional information sources:
Frederick, A. Bruce, Gymnastic Action Cards, Burgess Publishing Company, Minneapolis, Minnesota, 1965.
Barratt, Marcia, et al., Foundations for Movement, W. C. Brown Co., Dubuque, Iowa, 1964.

1. ROLL CALL

2. ACTIVITY PREPARATION

3. RELATED ACTIVITY COMMENTARY

4. THE ACTIVITY

5. DISMISSAL

———————————

Additional information sources:

November 1 to December 23

1. ROLL CALL

   a. Work on .. right face .. left face .. about face .. at ease
   b. March to the exercise formation.

2. ACTIVITY PREPARATION

   a. Run in position
   b. General stretching exercises for the entire body.

3. RELATED ACTIVITY COMMENTARY

   Explain the meaning of such terms as: kip .. tuck .. pike ..
   layout .. front leaning rest .. spot. The most important word
   is spot, because it is necessary to anticipate the need for protection .. know how to spot, and give positive assurance to the
   performer that his safety is being provided for.

4. THE ACTIVITY

   The climbing rope .. do not proceed in any activity before be-
   ing ready. Rope burns can be nasty and falls worse
   The low bar .. a few simple routines
   The parallel bars .. a few simple routines
   The vaults .. a few simple routines
   Use mats and be sure to carry back to hooks after the activities.

5. DISMISSAL

   Care for those that may have a few bruises. If the coordination
   of the individual seems impossible, assign something where the
   boy has a chance for success without danger.

Additional information sources:
Ruff, Wesley K., Gymnastics, Beginner to Competitor, W.C. Brown
Company, Dubuque, Iowa, 1959.
Fleishman, Edwin A., The Structure and Measurement of Physical
Fitness, Prentice-Hall, Inc., Englewood Cliffs, New Jersey, 1964.

1. ROLL CALL

2. ACTIVITY PREPARATION

3. RELATED ACTIVITY COMMENTARY

4. THE ACTIVITY

5. DISMISSAL

Additional information sources:

No. 3.

LATE WINTER

****

January 1 to March 15

1. ROLL CALL

    a. Note any burned out bulbs in the gym. Report to maintenance men.
    b. If an exit light is broken in play, also report, and get light guard.

2. ACTIVITY PREPARATION

    a. Give four strength building exercises
    b. Encourage for maximum effort .. note if a record.

3. RELATED ACTIVITY COMMENTARY

    Explain the use of heavy cotton sash cord for lariat twirling. How the ends are whipped. How the loop (honda) is made. The stem of the rope must be turned in the fingers as often as the loop rotates. One minute earns an A. A. A. point.

4. THE ACTIVITY

    Have a strand of rope for at least every 3 boys. Help individually getting the rope going. Encourage such progress as twirling in the vertical position. Watch out for lasso stunts. These could cause injury.

    A complicated relay adds spice to the end of the activity period that has not required much physical effort. Try this:
    Run to the end of the gym and remove one shoe. Return, touch the wall and again run to the end of the gym and remove the other shoe. Return, touch the wall and in turn remove both sox. When all members of the team have their shoes and sox at the other end, all get their shoes and sox and go to the dressing room.

5. DISMISSAL

    a. Caution about leaving the gym area before the signal
    b. Be sure to get the group to their next class on time.

Additional information sources:
Donnely, Richard, et al., Active Games and Contests, Ronald Press, New York, N.Y., 1958.

1. ROLL CALL

2. ACTIVITY PREPARATION

3. RELATED ACTIVITY COMMENTARY

4. THE ACTIVITY

5. DISMISSAL

_____

Additional information sources:

January 1 to March 15

1. ROLL CALL . . gym in use . . basement 40 x 60 is area assigned to conduct the class

    a. Line up on long wall on north side and call roll as usual
    b. Be patient with those who did not see notice of change of site for class, and do not complain.

2. ACTIVITY PREPARATION

    a. 30 straddle jumps
    b. 30 bending exercises to touch the opposite toe
    c. 25 pushups.

3. RELATED ACTIVITY COMMENTARY

    Explain how to care for the injured. How the injured should and should not be carried. The three-man lift where there is an emergency and possible back injury. Explain other carries.

4. THE ACTIVITY

    a. One carries one the length of room, then the boys reverse. This must not be a race. Be sure that the lifting is done with no harm to those lifting. The boys should be paired off rather evenly insofar as weight and apparent strength is concerned. Use fireman's carry.

    b. Two carry one. The two make a chair of their hands and the one places his arms around the necks of the carriers. All three should get a round trip ride. Again, no race.

    c. Three carry one. Make the pick up from the floor. Teach the count of three and all lift together. All make the round trip. Sell the idea that an injury can be aggravated by the wrong carry.

5. DISMISSAL

    If the area is far from the dressing room, allow more time.

1. <u>ROLL CALL</u>

2. <u>ACTIVITY PREPARATION</u>

3. <u>RELATED ACTIVITY COMMENTARY</u>

4. <u>THE ACTIVITY</u>

5. <u>DISMISSAL</u>

_____

Additional information sources:

January 1 to March 15

1. ROLL CALL

    a. Check on boys returning after illness for medical clear-
        ance from physician
    b. Be prepared to have restricted activity for those that seem
        not up to par.

2. ACTIVITY PREPARATION

    a. 5 minutes of endurance exercises
    b. 3 minutes of muscular strength building exercises
    c. Leap frog around the gym two times. Three paces between
        each squatter.

3. RELATED ACTIVITY COMMENTARY

    Explain weight lifting and the idea of gradually adding weight
    and the number of times each act is performed. Tell the story
    about the Greek boy Milo who went out into the pasture to get
    a baby bull calf. He did it every day for three years (?) Dem-
    onstrate proper form and the dangers of the showoff.

4. THE ACTIVITY

    Divide groups in areas where they can work on individual interests
    a. Weight lifting .. followed by 150 rope skips
    b. Shuffleboard (for boys returning from sickness)
    c. Handball
    d. Badminton tourney .. doubles
    e. One-half floor basketball.

5. DISMISSAL

    Again note condition of boys who have been on the sick list.

Additional information sources:
Milton, John E., "Weight Training in the Physical Education Program,"
Athletic Journal, September, 1963.
The Athletic Institute, Chicago, Illinois has published a series of
booklets entitled "How to Improve Your Sports."

1. ROLL CALL

2. ACTIVITY PREPARATION

3. RELATED ACTIVITY COMMENTARY

4. THE ACTIVITY

5. DISMISSAL

———————

Additional information sources:

January 1 to March 15

1. ROLL CALL

    a. Add or subtract new names from the roll, if the class personnel changes.
    b. If some boys have very many absences, ascertain the cause.

2. ACTIVITY PREPARATION

    a. Give one strength building exercise, one stretching exercise, and one exercise for developing endurance.
    b. Allow an opportunity to get A. A. A. point by jumping over the foot, held with one hand. Jumper must not lose his balance.

3. RELATED ACTIVITY COMMENTARY

    Explain the use of heavy cotton sash cord for rope skipping. Demonstrate moving the feet on a two-beat. Left, left, then right, right. Then, crossing the hands left and right. The same type of rope for lariat work may be used, but possibly time would indicate that this be reserved for another period.

4. THE ACTIVITY

    Have a strand of rope for at least every three boys. Work on the two beat. Fifty successful jumps with a left and right cross is pretty good for the first period of rope work. Encourage practice in spare time. 150 turns with a left and right cross would give an A. A. A. point.

5. DISMISSAL

    a. How clean are the clean towels?
    b. How clean is the rest of the clothing that is being worn for class?

Additional information sources:
Clarke, H. Harrison., Application of Measurement to Health and Physical Education, Prentice-Hall, Inc.,1959.
Wallis, Earl and Logan, Gene A., Figure Improvement and Body Conditioning Through Exercise, Prentice-Hall, Inc., New York, N.Y., 1964.

1. ROLL CALL

2. ACTIVITY PREPARATION

3. RELATED ACTIVITY COMMENTARY

4. THE ACTIVITY

5. DISMISSAL

―――――――

Additional information sources:

January 1 to March 15 .. Gym not available

1. ROLL CALL

    a. Count off on longest wall of old assembly hall. If 20 per cent of the class is absent for other activities, be sure to verify excuses

    b. Do not complain to the class about the absences. Showing displeasure of administration of the activities causing the small class is in bad taste and accomplishes little.

2. ACTIVITY PREPARATION

    a. 25 straddle jumps
    b. 25 assisted situps
    c. 25 squat thrusts.

3. RELATED ACTIVITY COMMENTARY

Games involving imitation of animals are common activities for nights of fun. They can be used by the student in the event when some time he is in charge of a club or church program.

4. THE ACTIVITY

    a. Monkey walk .. one walks on all fours, two wraps legs around one, and holds one by his buttocks
    b. Rooster walk .. a single. Merely hold on to ankles
    c. Bunny hop .. This is all fours, just imitate a rabbit
    d. Duck walk .. arms folded. (See commentary on this in definition of exercises as to purpose)
    e. Horse back .. one merely hops on back of two. Use boys of like size
    f. Horse walk .. one on all fours. Two lays on back one and holds on to ankles, legs around the body of one
The list is only limited by the imagination of the instructor.

5. DISMISSAL

Caution again about running on slippery floors.

Additional information sources:
Neilson, N.P. and Van Hagen, Winifred, Physical Education for Elementary Schools, The Ronald Press, New York., 1956.

1. ROLL CALL

2. ACTIVITY PREPARATION

3. RELATED ACTIVITY COMMENTARY

4. THE ACTIVITY

5. DISMISSAL

_____

Additional information sources:

January 1 to March 15

1. ROLL CALL

Start on time .. if delayed by telephone, etc., try to get class going with a student leader. This does not have to occur too frequently to become a problem.

2. ACTIVITY PREPARATION

a. 15 squat thrusts
b. Run in position 60 seconds. Knees high
c. 15 bellyrockers
d. Stretching exercises

3. RELATED ACTIVITY COMMENTARY

Explain the use of continuities for teaching skills in basketball .. demonstrate the screen .. the pivot.

4. THE ACTIVITY

Four corner screen drill   Four corner drill for pivot

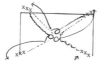
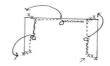

X dribbles two steps and passes to his right. The receiver waits until X goes by him and does the same. This works to the left, also. After 10 or 12 minutes, one-half floor scrimmage.

X dribbles to the center, pivots on his left foot and passes to the boy in the next corner. He follows his pass. The receiver does likewise.

5. DISMISSAL

Check for foot blisters

_____

Additional information sources:
Note: The many basketball coaching books on the market will furnish ideas for drills.

1. ROLL CALL

2. ACTIVITY PREPARATION

3. RELATED ACTIVITY COMMENTARY

4. THE ACTIVITY

5. DISMISSAL

_____

Additional information sources:

January 1 to March 15

1. ROLL CALL

    Note that almost half of the class is absent due to a science field
    trip.

2. ACTIVITY PREPARATION

    a. General loosening up exercises
    b. Use student leader that seldom has leadership opportunities.

3. RELATED ACTIVITY COMMENTARY

    Explain the simple rules for the game of Black Eye. Any number
    may play, but the ideal is about ten to a side. Played like base-
    ball, except hitter throws at the "batter" who has his buttocks
    up at the free throw line. Pitcher is in center circle. A flinch
    on the part of the batter, a discernable movement as a result of
    the ball passing close to him, is an out. The instructor deter-
    mines the flinches and the tag outs from a position on the side-
    line. See text for more detailed game layout.

4. THE ACTIVITY

    The passing game will get more OUTS. Sitting on the sideline
    in batting order speeds up the play. The throw that strikes the
    runner should be made with two hands. The only apparent danger
    would be impeding the runner, which is illegal, and striking
    the runner in the ear. The soft tag is encouraged, because
    more runners can be caught in one play.

5. DISMISSAL

    Note enthusiasm for game. This should determine how soon
    this activity should be repeated. The locker room will tend to
    determine how the other activities are going, also.

Additional information sources:
Sapora, Allen V. and Mitchell, Elmer D., The Theory of Play and
Recreation, The Ronald Press, New York, N.Y., 3rd edition., 1961.

1. ROLL CALL

2. ACTIVITY PREPARATION

3. RELATED ACTIVITY COMMENTARY

4. THE ACTIVITY

5. DISMISSAL

_____

Additional information sources:

January 1 to March 15

JOINT CLASS WITH GIRLS

1. <u>ROLL CALL</u>

   a. Have the roll call in the dressing room, it might avoid em-barrassment and speed things up
   b. Street clothes with possible exception of shoes.

2. <u>ACTIVITY PREPARATION</u>

   Bulletin board announcement that the class will be Square Dancing.

3. <u>RELATED ACTIVITY COMMENTARY</u>

   A dry run on the square dance figures should have been walked through previous to this meeting. Sell the idea of the social benefits of square dancing.

4. <u>THE ACTIVITY</u>

   a. Square dancing to records
   b. Let those who have danced before give a demonstration of the figures
   c. Walk through all figures. Keep them simple and try to learn one in one class
   d. This must be carefully worked out with the woman physical education instructor ahead of time.

5. <u>DISMISSAL</u>

   a. May be from the gym, unless shoes have to be taken back to the dressing room
   b. Find out if there is parental enthusiasm for square dancing and explore the possibility of a parent student party.

Additional information sources:
Hoctor Dance Records, Inc., Waldwick, New Jersey, lists dozens of 33 1/2 RPM records covering Folk Dancing, Square Dancing, Modern Dance, and music related activities.
See local record shop and adult square dance clubs.

1. <u>ROLL</u> <u>CALL</u>

2. <u>ACTIVITY</u> <u>PREPARATION</u>

3. <u>RELATED</u> <u>ACTIVITY</u> <u>COMMENTARY</u>

4. <u>THE</u> <u>ACTIVITY</u>

5. <u>DISMISSAL</u>

Additional information sources:

January 1 to March 15

1. ROLL CALL

    a. Walk the line and look for clothing variations
    b. Be sure that clothing is identified.

2. ACTIVITY PREPARATION

    a. Run in position 10 seconds .. 4 pushups and repeat 4 or 5
        times
    b. 12 situps with partner helping
    c. 10 squat thrusts
    d. Sprint one-half of floor, jog to wall, and repeat.

3. RELATED ACTIVITY COMMENTARY

    Explain specialized activities open to those interested, such as
    weight lifting, striking bag, juggling, fencing, gymnastics, or
    other things that might be logically associated with physical ed-
    ucation. Emphasize the responsibilities attached to the possible
    lessened supervision.

4. THE ACTIVITY

    a. Set up an indoor obstacle course. Under tables, up and over
        steps, zig zag run through eight or ten chairs, crawl under
        objects with less than a foot of clearance. The facilities at
        hand will determine the course of the run. Use a watch and
        give recognition to good performances.
    b. Check on those doing specialized and unsupervised events.

5. DISMISSAL

    a. Are towels clean?
    b. Encourage good locker housekeeping
    c. Encourage use of powder for chafing in thigh.

Additional information sources:
Ryser, Otto E., A Teacher's Manual for Tumbling and Apparatus Stunts,
W.C. Brown Co., Dubuque, Iowa, 1961.

1. <u>ROLL</u> <u>CALL</u>

2. <u>ACTIVITY</u> <u>PREPARATION</u>

3. <u>RELATED</u> <u>ACTIVITY</u> <u>COMMENTARY</u>

4. <u>THE</u> <u>ACTIVITY</u>

5. <u>DISMISSAL</u>

_____

Additional information sources:

January 1 to March 15

1. ROLL CALL

    a. Remind student leaders to check carefully on reasons for being absent
    b. Be alert to any signs of communicable disease .. mumps, etc.

2. ACTIVITY PREPARATION

    a. Run in position three thirty second periods. Try for increased count on each timing
    b. Do situps for thirty seconds. Try for increased count on each timing
    c. Do pushups for thirty seconds. Try for increased count on each timing.

3. RELATED ACTIVITY COMMENTARY

    Call attention to the advertisements that purport to make strong men out of weaklings in a limited amount of time .. the self-defense advertisements .. their cost ..

4. THE ACTIVITY

    a. Badminton
    b. Striking bag
    c. Weight lifting
    d. Shuffleboard
    e. Swimming unit
    f. Trampoline
    g. Gymnastic group prepares for exhibition with band background.

5. DISMISSAL

    Call attention to those who have failed to return checked out equipment, or did not report equipment which was broken during the course of play. There should be no penalty or reprimand for this, but it must be reported to the instructor.

Additional information sources:
Wells, Katharine, F., Posture Exercise Handbook -- A Progressive Sequence Approach, The Ronald Press, New York, N.Y., 1963.

No. 4.

SPRING

****

March 15 to June

1. ROLL CALL

    a. Call the roll outside. Try to have a constant area for calling roll, one that can easily be reached
    b. Keep the roster on a clipboard. Visual indication of the recording of their presence is desirable.

2. ACTIVITY PREPARATION

    a. Once around the track .. 440 yards .. allow two minutes
    b. 25 straddle jumps
    c. 10 bellyrockers
    d. 15 squat thrusts
    e. Free stretching and full trunk twists.

3. RELATED ACTIVITY COMMENTARY

    Explain parts of a test to measure probable ability in certain areas. The test might include the 50 yard dash for speed .. 880 for endurance .. shot put for strength and agility .. high jump for spring and special coordination .. broad jump for speed and spring .. Other activities may be added at discretion of instructor.

4. THE ACTIVITY

    a. It may take three to five periods to run off all of the events
    b. Keep accurate records and place top rankings on bulletin boards
    c. Watch for excessive fatigue in the 880
    d. Use a personnel sheet for the orderly conduct of the events
    e. Encourage outstanding performers to consider varsity team participation. Introduce them to the coaches.

5. DISMISSAL

    a. Wash out cinder bruises
    b. Cuts and skin punctures might indicate tetanus protection. If in doubt, consult a physician.

Additional information sources:
Calisch, Richard and Wallack, Jr., Lester C., Teaching Track and Field, The Interstate Printers and Publishers, Inc., Danville, Illinois, 1960.

1. ROLL CALL

2. ACTIVITY PREPARATION

3. RELATED ACTIVITY COMMENTARY

4. THE ACTIVITY

5. DISMISSAL

_____

Additional information sources:

PERSONNEL ASSIGNMENTS FOR THE CONDUCT OF TRACK TESTS

50 yards   Starter _____ Timers, each have a watch

1. _____ 2. _____ 3. _____

Clerk _____ Get list of runners early

880 yards   Starter _____ Timers, each have a watch

1. _____ 2. _____ 3. _____

Clerk _____ Get list of runners early

High Jump   Bar and standards _____ _____

Clerk _____ Get list of jumpers early
Have separate trials for obviously low jumpers.   Move
the bar up as fast as the abilities would indicate

Shot put   Clerk _____ Get list of putters early

Tape _____ _____
Caution: Carry the shot back to the circle.   Give specific
instructions that no try be made until the command is
given by the clerk

Running
Broad jump   Judge and clerk _____ Note scratches

Tape _____ _____
Call distances clearly to the clerk

Standing
Broad jump   Judge and clerk _____ Watch toeline

Tape _____ _____
While this is usually not a part of the standard field events
it still does have value in measuring spring without the
aid of a running start

    Be sure that the tests are well administered and that the personnel
doing the testing have been thoroughly briefed before they start work.
Carefully explain the rules for each event.   Post the scores of those
ranking high

NOTES:

March 15 to June

1. <u>ROLL CALL</u> .. stay inside .. bad weather

   a. Last quarter begins, check for class changes
   b. Appoint new squad leaders.

2. <u>ACTIVITY PREPARATION</u>

   a. Exercises peculiar to track activities
   b. General loosening up exercises for those not to work on the hurdle steps and the high jump.

3. <u>RELATED ACTIVITY COMMENTARY</u>

   Diagram the desired steps and form for both the high hurdles and the low hurdles. Develop form on two or three spaced hurdles. If the hurdler can not get over three in good form, he will never make ten. Show the steps in the approach for the high jump, and the forms that seem to bring greatest success to the champions.

4. <u>THE ACTIVITY</u>

   a. Work on high jump form with mats. Keep height of bar between three and four feet. Keep mats well placed to avoid injury
   b. Space out a few flights of both high and low hurdles as conditions will allow. Work on steps. Be sure the high hurdlers have had sufficient pre-trial stretching activities
   c. Have tennis unit work on a wall, if one is available and does not conflict
   d. Gymnasts who have positive spotters may work on their specialities.

5. <u>DISMISSAL</u>

   Note knee bruises .. and mat burns.

Additional information sources:
Healey, William A., <u>Physical Education Demonstrations Made Easy</u>,
The Interstate Printers and Publishers, Inc., Danville, Illinois,, 1962.

1. ROLL CALL

2. ACTIVITY PREPARATION

3. RELATED ACTIVITY COMMENTARY

4. THE ACTIVITY

5. DISMISSAL

———————————

Additional information sources:

March 15 to June

1. ROLL CALL

    a. Call the roll outside
    b. If the weather is chilly, note if boys are adequately clothed.

2. ACTIVITY PREPARATION

    a. Once around the track .. walk 50 steps .. run 100 steps ..
    b. Free stretching .. exercises designed to increase a leg split
    c. Run in position.

3. RELATED ACTIVITY COMMENTARY

    Explain the form for low hurdles and high hurdles. Emphasize the
    low hurdles and indicate that it will be the activity of the day. Ex-
    plain the steps between the barriers and the need for specialized
    exercise preparation.

4. THE ACTIVITY

    Set up as many flights of three hurdles as possible. Place them
    on grass. This avoids cinder injury. Encourage boys to get
    their steps to come out correctly, and then let them get on cinders.

    Part of the class may be on the tennis courts or the archery range.
    Insure adequate supervision.

    End hurdle session with a 880 yard run for A. A. A. point. 2:45

5. DISMISSAL

    a. Watch for bruises from hurdles or grass
    b. Boys should be encouraged to report injuries. Some hesitate,
        because they feel it is an attempt to get attention that would
        be ridiculed by other boys.

Additional information sources:
Bresnahan, George T. and Tuttle, W.W., Track and Field Athletics,
3rd edition., C.B. Mosby, St. Louis, Missouri, 1950.
Mortensen, Jess P. and Cooper, John M., Track and Field for Coach
and Athlete, Prentice-Hall, Inc., Englewood Cliffs, New Jersey, 1959.

1. <u>ROLL CALL</u>

2. <u>ACTIVITY</u> <u>PREPARATION</u>

3. <u>RELATED</u> <u>ACTIVITY</u> <u>COMMENTARY</u>

4. <u>THE</u> <u>ACTIVITY</u>

5. <u>DISMISSAL</u>

_____

Additional information sources:

March 15 to June .. outside

1. ROLL CALL

Note the ten boys who are excused and will be ten minutes late.

2. ACTIVITY PREPARATION

   a. Twice around the track. Walk fifty steps on the first lap
       and run fifty. Second lap, jog the distance
   b. Wet .. straddle jumps on the track .. bending exercises
       for maximum stretch.

3. RELATED ACTIVITY COMMENTARY

Discuss care of the feet. Proper fitting shoes and shoes fit for
the occasion. Keep wrinkles out of socks. Athletes foot, its
cause, its prevention, and methods of controlling it. Discuss
powder, the foot tub, and cautions to prevent its spread.

4. THE ACTIVITY

Tennis unit .. varsity boy makes a good assistant. See coach.
Number of courts limits the group that may be taught each day.
Every member of the class should have an opportunity to get
acquainted with as many activities as possible
Archery unit .. the above about tennis applies
Cross country .. walk and jog the course. Boys that show
more than average interest and aptitude should be encouraged
to see the coach of the sport involved.

5. DISMISSAL

   a. Watch for extra hot water coming through the shower heads
       as a result of cold water being diverted from the main line
       through the flushing of urinals and stools. This can be a
       dangerous form of the practical joker.

Additional information sources:
McKinney, Wayne C.: Archery, Johnson, Joan: Tennis, Nance, Virginia
L.: Golf. These are from a Physical Education Activities Series edited
by Aileene Lockhart. W.C. Brown Co., Dubuque, Iowa.

1. ROLL CALL

2. ACTIVITY PREPARATION

3. RELATED ACTIVITY COMMENTARY

4. THE ACTIVITY

5. DISMISSAL

Additional information sources:

March 15 to June

1. ROLL CALL .. Outside

   a. Speed up the calling of the roll
   b. Be sure boys are clothed for cool weather. Have warm cover nearby and handy for protection after having competed in exhausting events.

2. ACTIVITY PREPARATION

   a. Once around the track
   b. 12 pushups .. 12 bellyrockers .. 12 deep squats. Run in position 30 seconds .. stretching exercises of students choice for 3 minutes.

3. RELATED ACTIVITY COMMENTARY

   Explain and demonstrate the form for the shot put
   Explain and demonstrate the form and steps for the broad jump
   Explain and demonstrate the form for the discus
   Impress the dangers inherent in all three activities. Make safety rules and enforce them.

4. THE ACTIVITY

   Use three stations if the supervisory personnel is available for allowing the class to participate in the shot put .. broad jump .. discus. Have tapes and other materials on hand. Be sure that they are returned to the equipment room.

   Outdoor handball unit should work in their area.

5. DISMISSAL

   a. Be sure that all materials are returned to their proper place by an appointed committee
   b. Allow enough time for the boys to get back from the field to the dressing room. It may take a few minutes longer than usual if there is an additional distance factor.

Additional information sources:
Meyers, Carlton R. and Blesh, Erwin T., Measurement in Physical Education, The Ronald Press, New York, N.Y., 1962.

1. <u>ROLL</u> <u>CALL</u>

2. <u>ACTIVITY</u> <u>PREPARATION</u>

3. <u>RELATED</u> <u>ACTIVITY</u> <u>COMMENTARY</u>

4. <u>THE</u> <u>ACTIVITY</u>

5. <u>DISMISSAL</u>

———————

Additional information sources:

March 15 to June

1. ROLL CALL

   a. Call attention to the return of all school materials as the school year ends
   b. Be alert to spring fever tardiness.

2. ACTIVITY PREPARATION

   Five exercises involving .. strength building .. endurance .. stretching .. Do all in cadence.

3. RELATED ACTIVITY COMMENTARY

   Read the following article on sportsmanship. "If you are sportsmen, you will treat your rival a little better than yourself, then play hard and beat him if you can; and whether you beat him or not, you will do nothing in or before or after the game to forfeit his friendship or your own self-respect. No teammate, no captain, no coach, can be made responsible for your honor. In questions of fair and foul you are your own captain, your own coach, your whole team, and need never be defeated." (Address to Yale freshmen in "Men, Women, and Collegues." by LeBaron Russel Briggs, published by Houghton Mifflin and Co., Copyright 1925.)

4. THE ACTIVITY

   a. Finish incompleted tourneys that were started anytime during the year
   b. Unit in golf. Use 8 iron or other short distance club. More than normal caution is needed because of possible traffic on driving range. Encourage use of public course and have scores reported on the first time around.
   c. Nine over par or less qualifies for A. A. A. point.

5. DISMISSAL

   Again call attention that all school uniforms will be called in.

Additional information sources:
Bowling, Maurine, Tested Ways of Teaching Golf Classes, W. C. Brown Co., Dubuque, Iowa, 1964.

1. ROLL CALL

2. ACTIVITY PREPARATION

3. RELATED ACTIVITY COMMENTARY

4. THE ACTIVITY

5. DISMISSAL

———————————

Additional information sources:

March 15 to June .. last class to be dressed

1.   ROLL CALL .. outside

Walk the line and congratulate the class on their attendance
and interest.

2.   ACTIVITY PREPARATION

25 pushups .. give A. A. A. point if in good form
25 bellystretchers .. A. A. A. point if in good form
General loosening up exercises.

3.   RELATED ACTIVITY COMMENTARY

Detail a conditioning program during the summer months .. if
they are seniors outline an easy way to stay in condition. Maintain interest in tennis .. golf .. fishing .. bicycling. Watch
the diet. The need for good sleep habits. Call attention to
the recent findings on tobacco and alcohol.   Avoid a sermon.

4.   THE ACTIVITY

Last chance to run 880 in 2:45 or less
Last chance to run mile in 6:00 or less
Last chance to run 440 in 60 seconds or less
Last chance to broad jump 17 feet or more
Last chance to high jump 5 feet or more
Last chance to put the shot 33 feet or more
Last chance to run the 100 in 12 seconds or less
In this one period the boy should not be allowed to do more than
one of the exhausting running events.

5.   DISMISSAL

Collect all school clothing. Return deposits, if any.

_____

Additional information sources:
Johnson, Warren R., et al., Health Concepts for College Students,
The Ronald Press Company, New York, N.Y., (This is for adult
level reading.) 1962.

1. ROLL CALL

2. ACTIVITY PREPARATION

3. RELATED ACTIVITY COMMENTARY

4. THE ACTIVITY

5. DISMISSAL

_____

Additional information sources:

March 15 to June

1. ROLL CALL .. Street clothes

   a. Call roll inside
   b. Check on walking shoes.

2. ACTIVITY PREPARATION

   None.

3. RELATED ACTIVITY COMMENTARY

   Explain that the activity of the day will be a walk that must
   be done at about the rate of three to four miles an hour.
   Explain the course to be followed and the need to arrive back
   in school in time for an orderly DISMISSAL.

4. THE ACTIVITY

   Walk the required course. The instructor, if up to it, should go
   along. Flags, ribbons, or directional markers should be laid
   out before class. The course must be free from vehicular hazards. No hitchhiking, no shortcuts, and the group must within
   reason stay close together. This is not a race. No trotting.
   Three miles would seem a reasonable distance for an ordinary
   school period.

5. DISMISSAL

   a. Check for foot blisters
   b. Note excessive fatigue
   c. Account for those that come in later than would seem nec-
      essary.

Additional information sources:
Brightbill, Charles K., Man and Leisure: A Philosophy of Recreation,
Prentice-Hall, Inc., Englewood Cliffs, New Jersey, 1961.
President's Council on Youth Fitness. Youth Physical Fitness. United
States Government Printing Office, Washington, D.C., 1961.

1. <u>ROLL CALL</u>

2. <u>ACTIVITY PREPARATION</u>

3. <u>RELATED ACTIVITY COMMENTARY</u>

4. <u>THE ACTIVITY</u>

5. <u>DISMISSAL</u>

———————

Additional information sources:

March 15 to June .. last class

1. <u>ROLL</u> <u>CALL</u> .. inside

Walk the line and call attention to any school equipment that may still be out.

2. <u>ACTIVITY</u> <u>PREPARATION</u>

Each boy should have a couple of pencils with erasers.

3. <u>RELATED</u> <u>ACTIVITY</u> <u>COMMENTARY</u>

Explain the purpose of the all-sports and physical education test which covers material that a reasonably informed student should be able to answer. Instructor may use his own discretion in using it as a grading device. Probably best, not.

4. <u>THE</u> <u>ACTIVITY</u>

Spread the boys out on the gym floor. Give each boy his copy of the test and let him use the floor as his table. Keep the test within a reasonable time limit. Post the results of the best half of the test on the bulletin board, but make it known that others may find their grade in the instructor's office.

5. <u>DISMISSAL</u>

   a. Dismiss sufficiently early to take class for a tour of inspection of the locker room
   b. Note articles left behind in the lockers
   c. Note condition of locker doors and hooks for damage
   d. Take note of all missing materials reported
   e. Shake the hand of every boy in your class as he leaves.

Additional information sources:
Miller, Arthur G. and Massey, M. Dorothy, <u>A Dynamic Concept of Physical Education for</u> Secondary Schools, Prentice-Hall, Inc., Englewood Cliffs, New Jersey, 1963.
Neilson, N.P. and Bronson, Alice Oakes, <u>Problems in Physical Education: An Introductory Course</u>, Prentice-Hall, Inc., Englewood Cliffs, New Jersey, 1965.

1. <u>ROLL CALL</u>

2. <u>ACTIVITY PREPARATION</u>

3. <u>RELATED ACTIVITY COMMENTARY</u>

4. <u>THE ACTIVITY</u>

5. <u>DISMISSAL</u>

Additional information sources:

CHAPTER   III.

BASIC   EXERCISE   GROUPS   AS   TO   PURPOSE

A.   Isotonic Exercises Designed to Increase Muscle Strength

B.   Isometric Exercises Designed to Increase Muscle Strength

C.   Exercises Designed for Improving Muscle Endurance

D.   Muscle Stretching Exercises Designed for Body Flexibility

E.   General Conditioning Exercises

****

A.   ISOTONIC EXERCISES DESIGNED TO INCREASE
MUSCLE STRENGTH

The following exercises are designed to use additional
weight as a load factor by adding a partner's weight or by moving body parts through a greater range in opposition to gravity.

Students will vary in their basic level of strength for
different muscle groups and the instructor will have to use his
judgment in modifying the exercise for the entire class, or
classify certain students to exercise in a certain modified way.
For example, the better method of "loading," or providing resistance for the abdominal muscles, is to have the sit-ups performed with the trunk hyper-extended. This would be a type of
exercise where sit-ups are performed with the seat resting two
feet or more above the ground level, as one sitting on the back
of a partner who is on his hands and knees. However, students
with suspected weak abdominals should do this exercise with the
seat at ground level for fear of possible hernia occurrence if
the greater load is practiced.

In each exercise a time limit is established, depending on
the group, and this limit can also be adjusted to certain students
by extending or reducing the limit. A suggested limit is thirty
seconds. To gain strength the repetitions must increase after a
number of class periods has passed. If maximum speed of repetitions is achieved in the chosen time limit, then the time limit
should be increased. The purpose is to increase the speed of
repetitions until a maximum number is reached. This compri-
ses the overload, or progressive resistance.

An instructor may wish to increase the suggested exercise
period beyond that of thirty seconds. If this is contemplated, it
should be kept in mind that two or more students will have to go
through the same exercise and necessary time will have to be
allowed for the performance. Experience in administering the
exercises to a class will dictate the best changes to make concerning the time element.

GROUP I.   This exercise is designed for the flexor muscles
of the elbow and depressor muscles of the upper arm.

Figure 1

Figure 2

Exercise 1.   Chinning.

Arrangement: Students exercise in groups of three each,
selected as to similar height.

Starting Position: Two partners face, with the arms
straight and the hands resting on the other's shoulders, legs
spread sideward.   Third partner sits on the ground between
standing partners with the legs bent and crossed with the
hands grasping wrists above.

Exercise: On command, and for thirty seconds, the
sitting partner chins as fast as he can, noting the number ac-
complished.   Each partner rotates position.   (NOTE: The load
or resistance may be increased by the chinning partner holding
the legs at right angle to the trunk while executing the chin.)

GROUP II.   This exercise is designed for the extensor muscles of the upper leg.

Figure 1

Figure 2

Exercise 2.   Deep Squats.

Arrangement: Students exercise in groups of two, selected as to similar body weight.

Starting Position: The standing student supports his partner on his back.

Exercise: On command to start, the erect student squats as far down as he can and returns to the starting position. Thirty seconds are allowed for as many repetitions as possible, and the number is noted. Partners exchange positions and the exercise is repeated. (NOTE: An alternate exercise may be used for a lesser load factor. One partner lies on the back, knees against chest, lower legs vertical. The partner places his hands on the upright feet and sinks to the chest in push-up position. The exercise is for the lower partner to successively push the legs up straight and back to start position.)

121

GROUP III.   This exercise is designed for the flexor muscles of the upper arm and extensor muscles of the lower arm.

Figure 1

Figure 2

Exercise 3.   Vertical Push-ups.

Arrangement: Students exercise in groups of three each.

Starting Position: Two partners face each other, grasping the ankles of the third partner who kicks to a hand-stand position.

Exercise: On command, the hand-stand partner bends elbows until the top of head touches the ground, then he returns to starting position.   Thirty seconds are allowed and number of repetitions is noted.   Partners exchange positions. (NOTE: Two alternate positions may be used: #1 - in pairs, one partner lies on back, arms vertical. Upper partner places chest and hands on hands of lower partner, assuming a push-up position. Lower partner bends elbows, lowering the upper partner to the chest and returns him to starting position; #2 - the regular inclined position for push-ups may be utilized.

122

GROUP IV.   This exercise is designed for the flexor muscles located on the front of the trunk.

Figure 1

Figure 2

Exercise 4.   Three-man Sit-ups.

Arrangement: Students exercise in groups of three.

Starting Position: One partner assumes a position on the hands and knees. The exercising student sits on this person's back, while the third partner, from a kneeling squat, holds the sitting partner's feet.

Exercise: On command, the sitting partner leans backward touching the head gently to the ground and returns to the starting position.   Thirty seconds are allowed for greatest number of repetitions.   The number of repetitions is noted and partners exchange positions. (NOTE: Two alternate exercises may be used: #1 - same procedure as for Exercise 4, except partner who is on hands and knees lies flat; #2 - work in pairs in regular sit-up position.)

GROUP V.   This exercise is designed for the foot depressor muscles located in the lower leg.

Figure 1

Figure 2

Exercise 5.   Heel-lifts.

Arrangement: Students exercise in groups of two, selected as to similar weight.

Starting Position: The standing student supports his partner on his back.

Exercise: On command, the standing partner lifts the heels as high off the ground as he can with the toes remaining on the surface, and returns to starting position. The number of repetitions is noted for the exercise period of thirty seconds. (NOTE: If increased resistance is desired, a two-inch block of wood may be placed under the toes. If decreased load is desired, students may exercise single rather than double.)

GROUP VI.   This exercise is designed for the extensor
muscles of the back.

Figure 1

Figure 2

Exercise 6.   Back-lifts.

Arrangement: Students exercise in groups of three.

Starting Position: One student assumes a position on the
ground on hands and knees.   The exercising partner lies across
this partner's back, placing his thighs on the back with the face
close to the ground.   The third partner assumes a kneeling squat
and holds to the exercising partner's lower legs and heels.

Exercise: On command, the exercising student lifts his
upper body as high as he can, with the lower body parts suppor-
ted by the kneeling partner, and returns to the starting position.
Thirty seconds are allowed for greatest number of repetitions,
and then the partners exchange positions. (NOTE: Two variations may be used: #1 - the supporting partner may assume a
prone position instead of the hand-knee position; #2 - work in
pairs or singly without support.)

GROUP VII.   This exercise is designed for the lateral flexor muscles of the trunk located on the left side of the body.

Figure 1   Figure 2

Exercise 7.   Side-bender - Left.

Arrangement: Students exercise in groups of three.

Starting Position: One student assumes a position on the ground on his hands and knees. The exercising partner lies across this partner, resting the right hip on the back with the right ear close to the ground. The third partner assumes a kneeling squat position in order to support the exercising partner's legs.

Exercise: On command, the exercising partner raises the trunk laterally, with little or no forward flexion, as high as possible, and then returns to the starting position. The number of repetitions is noted in a time period of thirty seconds. The partners then exchange positions.

GROUP VIII.   This exercise is designed for the lateral flexor muscles of the trunk located on the right side of the body.

Figure 1

Figure 2

Exercise 8.   Side-bender - Right.

Arrangement: Students exercise in groups of three.

Starting Position: One student assumes a position on the ground on his hands and knees.   The exercising partner lies across his partner, resting the left hip on the back with the left ear close to the ground.   The third partner assumes a kneeling squat position in order to support the exercising partner's legs.

Exercise: On command, the exercising partner raises the trunk laterally, with little or no forward flexion, as high as possible, and then returns to the starting position.   The number of repetitions is noted in a time period of thirty seconds.   The partners then exchange positions.

B.   ISOMETRIC EXERCISES DEGISNED TO INCREASE
MUSCLE STRENGTH.

In order to approximate the increases in muscle strength
through isometric contractions, the maximum strength should be
measured and two-thirds of this load used and held for a period
of six seconds. In a class situation, however, in the absence of
instruments to so measure the effort, a less valid method may
have to be utilized. This method would be to instruct the students to exert maximum effort in each of the exercises for the
time specified.

Isometric Exercises for Class Situations. The use of
isometric exercises in a class situation may be of doubtful value,
particularly when isotonic exercises can be used instead. However, there may be some instances where isometric exercises
would be advantageous.

For a class situation, one might apply the isometric
method of exercising to those exercises listed earlier in the
text for improving strength through isotonic exercise. In each
instance, the isotonic exercise movement would be halted at the
half-way mark and then held for a period of six seconds. For
example, the chinning exercise would be performed and halted
half-way through the range of motion, and held for six seconds.
The same technique could be applied to the remainder of the
isotonic exercises.

Isometric Exercises for Purposes Other Than Class
Situations. There are many instances, among class members
as well as varsity team members, where it is desirable to
attempt rehabilitation of some previous muscle injury. Isometric exercises will aid in the improvement of strength, and have
the advantage that they can be done with little space or equipment. Consequently, these exercises can be done at home, and
can be repeated several times during a twenty-four hour period.

In addition to the use of isometric exercises for injury rehabilitation, the exercises may be used by regular class members for "home" conditioning of muscle tissue. Since it is established that isometric exercises will improve strength, many young people of a class might be motivated to set up a conditioning program of their own at home. In a matter of only a few moments, in the isolation of one's room, the exercises could be performed several times a day.

For whatever purpose one might choose, the following exercises are given as a guide, with the suggestion that any particular muscle group may be worked in a similar manner.

<u>Neck Exercises</u>: Place the hands on the front of the head and tilt the head to the rear. Hold the head in this position firmly with the hands and attempt to press the head forward against this resistance (Figure 1). In opposition to the position just described, place the hands on the back of the head and attempt to move the head backward against resistance (Figure 2). With the head tilted to the left (Figure 3) and then to the right (Figure 4), attempt to press against the resistance provided by the hands. Exert all pressures against resistance for a period of six to ten seconds and repeat each twice.

Figure 1

Figure 3

Figure 2

Figure 4

Elbow Flexor Exercise: Place the left hand in front of the body so that the lower arm is at a right angle to the upper arm. Place the right hand on the left wrist (Figure 5). While holding the lower arm in this position, try to bring the left hand up toward the chin. Exert pressure for six to ten seconds and repeat twice. Exchange position of the arms and hand and repeat the exercise.

While this exercise is described as an elbow flexor exercise, it may readily be seen that the extensor muscles of the opposite arm are being used to prevent the upward movement of the elbow which is in the process of being flexed. Thus, both the flexor and the extensor muscles of the elbows are being exercised.

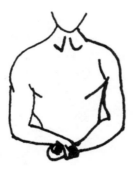

Figure 5

Quadriceps Exercise: The three vasti muscles along with the rectus femoris comprise the group of muscles known as the quadriceps. When a knee has been injured, and in many cases after surgical operations, this group of muscles receives prominent attention in rehabilitation exercise programs. While this is as it should be, it also should be remembered that this group of muscles cross only the anterior portion of the knee joint. Consequently, there are other groups of muscles that also should be exercised when rehabilitation exercises are to be given. By reversing the action given for exercising the quadriceps, the flexors

130

of the knee located on the posterior side of the knee joint may be exercised. For the quadriceps exercise, the left toe is placed behind the right ankle (Figure 6). Pressure is exerted by the left leg for a period of six to ten seconds, and then repeated twice. Leg positions are exchanged and the exercise repeated.

Figure 6

Leg Adductors Exercise: This exercise is designed for the group of muscles located on the inside of the upper leg. These muscles are those that pull the legs together from a wide spread position, as in the completion of the frog kick in swimming the breaststroke. The abductor group of muscles may be exercised by placing the outside of the foot against some stationary object like a table leg, or wall, and pressing the foot hard against it.

The exercises involving these muscle groups are not particularly helpful toward stabilizing the knee joint, since both groups are primarily inserted above the knee on the femur. Such exercises, however, might prove of some value to those students who are engaged in such sports activities as swimming, or running hurdles in track events.

For the leg adductors exercise, the student assumes a standing position. The left knee is bent with the middle third of the lower leg placed against the right knee (Figure 7). Pressure is exerted by the left leg for a period of six to ten seconds, and repeated twice. The positions of the legs are exchanged and the exercise repeated.

Figure 7

From the examples of isometric exercises demonstrated above, one can see how easy it is to improvise similar exercises wherein little or no equipment is needed. The student himself may devise exercises of his own, if he so desires.

It should be pointed out that initial testing for strength of various muscle groups would be most desirable. Such initial measurements would be compared with later measurements and the amount of gain in strength could be accurately determined.

C. EXERCISES DESIGNED FOR IMPROVING MUSCLE ENDURANCE.

Before exercises are put into a class situation the instructor should be aware of the purpose of such exercises. Then, if the purpose fits in with the objectives and time element, the exercises will prove quite beneficial.

Muscular endurance may be defined as that characteristic of muscle tissue which allows it to work with an optimum load over a comparatively long period of time. This differs with muscle strength which may be defined as that characteristic of muscle tissue which allows it to work briefly with a comparatively heavy load.

One exercise program may lead to increased muscle strength and a lesser increase in muscle endurance. Another exercise program may be designed to lead to an increase in muscle endurance with a lesser increase in muscle strength. An example in chinning might be used in illustration, where two boys are exercising and each has a different objective. One boy chins using progressive resistance. In this approach he keeps the number of chins at a maximum of about twelve, and when this point is reached he adds more weight to his body and repeats the process. Eventually he may be able to chin with a hundred pounds attached to his feet. The second boy chins with the objective of achieving a hundred chins with no increased weight added. If each boy achieved his objective and tried to duplicate the other's feat, he would be disappointed, since each was conditioning the muscle tissue for different objectives.

Running events in track may lend themselves to the same sort of analysis if one can conceive of the idea of omitting references to the complicated mechanism of cardio-respiratory functions and of incurrence of an oxygen debt. The 100-yard dash requires a great deal of muscle strength to move the body parts at a very high rate for a time period of ten seconds, or less.

This same abundance of muscle strength is not necessary to cover the two-mile distance where the rate of movement is much slower. The running of sprints is associated with the progressive resistance approach to building muscle strength, while running the distance events is associated with the muscle endurance approach. It is interesting to observe the normal body types usually associated with each of the sprints and distance events. The sprinter is quite muscular and it may be hypothesized that muscular men make better sprinters, or that sprinting makes the man muscular.

The concept for building muscle endurance as an aid to a greater athletic performance in swimming has been written about in another source.[1] Swimming a competitive distance of 200 yards or more at a rapid cadence requires a high degree of muscle endurance and not so much strength. In this study the exercises were recorded on tape, with the movements simulating strokes, and the tempo was set for proper cadence.

If the objective of exercising in a class situation to achieve muscle endurance seems worthwhile, one must be prepared to allot more time to these exercises than for other types. It is necessary, also, to establish a rhythmical beat for each exercise with the cadence placed at moderate to above-moderate speed and compatible with the time span.

The following exercises are of the calisthenics type familiar to most physical educators. Each exercise should be performed, however, at a moderately fast and consistent rhythm for a period of two minutes or more. When a student can no longer exercise to the established cadence, he should stop and on subsequent days attempt to improve his ability to stay longer with the cadence.

---

[1] Groves, William H., "Dry Land Workout for Swimmers." Journal of Health, Physical Education, and Recreation, AAHPER, 37:4:72-73, April, 1966.

GROUP I.   This exercise is designed for improving muscle
endurance of the abductor and adductor muscles of both the upper
arms and legs.

Figure 1

Figure 2

Exercise 1.   Side Straddle Hops.

Arrangement: Students exercise in individual alignment.

Starting Position: The students assume an erect position,
standing at attention.

Exercise: On the count of one, the hands are brought
directly overhead with the arms kept straight, while at the same
time the legs are spread wide to either side. On the count of
two, the hands and legs are brought back to the starting position
of attention.

GROUP II.   This exercise is designed for the elevator and depressor muscles of the upper arm and the flexor and extensor muscles of the upper leg.

Figure 1

Figure 2

Exercise 2.   Front Straddle Hops.

Arrangement: Students exercise in individual alignment.

Starting Position: The students assume an erect position, standing at attention.

Exercise: On the count of one, the left arm and right leg move forward as the right arm and left leg move backward. On the count of two, the movements of the arms and legs are reversed.

GROUP III.   This exercise is designed for the flexor and extensor muscles of the trunk.

Figure 1   Figure 2

Exercise 3. Toe-Touch Swing.

Arrangement: Students exercise in individual alignment.

Starting Position: The students assume an erect position standing with the legs together and hands stretched overhead.

Exercise: On the count of one, the arms are kept straight and swung down and forward until the hands touch the toes. On the count of two, the body returns to the starting position.

GROUP IV.   This exercise is designed for the flexor and extensor muscles of both the hands and feet.

Figure 1

Figure 2

Exercise 4.   Hand-Foot Wave.

   Arrangement: Students exercise in individual alignment.

   Starting Position: The students assume a sitting position. The legs are straight with the toes pointed forward as far as they will go.   The arms are held straight out from the shoulders. The palms of the hands face downward and back toward the body as far as they will go.

   Exercise: On the count of one, the toes are brought back toward the body along with the hands as far as they will go, while at the same time the arms and legs remain straight.   On the count of two, the hands and feet return to the starting position.

GROUP V.   This exercise is designed for the abdominal group of muscles that assist in twisting the trunk on the pelvis.

Figure 1   Figure 2   Figure 3

Exercise 5.   Trunk-Twister.

Arrangement: Students exercise in individual alignment.

Starting Position: The students assume a standing position. The legs and arms are spread wide to either side.

Exercise: On the count of one, the trunk bends forward and twists to the right with the left hand touching the right toe. On the count of two, the body returns to the starting position. The trunk is twisted to the opposite side on counts three and four. (NOTE: Fig. 1 shows the starting position and is the same position for counts 2 and 4. Fig. 2 shows the position for count 1, while Fig. 3 shows the position for count 3.)

GROUP VI.   This exercise is designed for the extensor muscles of the arms, legs, and back.

Figure 1

Figure 2

Exercise 6.   Back Archer.

Arrangement: Students exercise in individual alignment.

Starting Position: The students assume a position lying
face down on the ground. The legs are extended straight to the
rear. The arms may be stretched out straight overhead, or
they may be bent with the hands placed behind the head.

Exercise: On the count of one, the chest and legs are
lifted as high as possible off the ground, forming an arch to the
back. On the count of two, the body returns to the starting
position.

GROUP VII.   This exercise is designed for the extensor muscles of the upper and lower legs.

Figure 1

Figure 2

Exercise 7.   Squat Jumps.

Arrangement: Students exercise in individual alignment.

Starting Position: The students assume a deep squat
position.   One foot is placed about eighteen inches ahead of the
other foot.   The hands are placed behind the neck.

Exercise: On the count of one, the student jumps up into
the air with the body erect.   While in the air the feet reverse
position in preparation for the landing.   On the count of two, a
jump into the air is again made with the feet reversing position.
On each landing the body sinks to a deep squat.

GROUP VIII.   This exercise is designed for all the muscles that surround the shoulder joint.

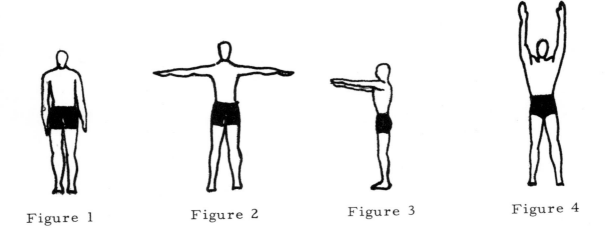

Figure 1   Figure 2   Figure 3   Figure 4

Exercise 8.   Eight-Count Arm Swing.

Arrangement: Students exercise in individual alignment.

Starting Position: The students assume an erect position, standing with the hands vertically at the side.

Exercise: On the indicated count number, the arms move to the following positions: One, to side-horizontal; Two, to front-horizontal; Three, to side-horizontal; Four, straight over-head; Five, to side-horizontal; Six, to front-horizontal; Seven, to side-horizontal; and Eight, back to starting position.
(NOTE: Fig. 1 shows the starting position and count 8; Fig. 2 shows counts 1, 3, 5 and 7; Fig. 3 shows the counts of 2 and 6; and Fig. 4 shows count 4.)

D.   MUSCLE STRETCHING EXERCISES DESIGNED FOR
BODY FLEXIBILITY

One characteristic of "old age" is the apparent inflexibility
of body parts. Young people, while not approaching old age inflexibility, vary among themselves with some being much less
inflexible than others.

The more flexible the body parts the less chance for injury
when a maximum range of motion is suddenly applied. Muscle
under a high degree of tonus tends to limit the range of motion.
Consequently, the young muscular adult needs to practice flexibility exercises. He should, in particular, pre-stretch muscles
prior to making an all-out muscular effort.

An increase in flexibility will allow body parts to acceler-
ate over a longer distance, thus improving power out-put so
necessary in skills calling for "explosive" effort. The baseball
pitcher, for example, can improve the speed of his fast ball by
increasing the range of extension of the throwing hand. A place-
kicker in football can achieve greater distances if he will increase
the range of the femur in extension just prior to kicking the ball.
These are but two of many examples indicating the value in sports
skills of flexibility.

The following exercises are designed to use some force on
one or more body parts to stretch the muscles and ligaments in
the direction opposite of normal action. The group of muscles
being stretched, or elongated, should not be contracted. Some
pain will occur and the individual undergoing the stretching must
decide when the force should be discontinued. The person who is
exerting the force on a partner should do so with caution.

Three attempts should be made, preferably, to stretch the
muscles involved in the exercise, with each full effort held for
a period of six to ten seconds.

143

GROUP I.   This exercise is designed to stretch the flexor muscles of the hands.

Figure 1

Figure 2

Exercise 1.   Hand Extensor.

Arrangement: Students exercise in individual alignment.

Starting Position: The student assumes a position with the knees on the ground, toes pointed to the rear. The palms of the hands are placed flat on the ground, fingers pointing toward the knees. The buttocks are lowered six to eight inches above the heels.

Exercise: On command, lower and move the buttocks backward to sit on the heels. The palms of the hands should retain their flat contact with the ground. This position is held for six to ten seconds and repeated twice.

GROUP II.   This exercise is designed to extend the pelvis on the femur. When this is done, the rectus femoris muscle is put on a stretch. If the femur is lowered enough the vasti muscles are also stretched.

Figure 1

Figure 2

Exercise 2.   Layback.

Arrangement: Students exercise in individual alignment.

Starting Position: The student assumes a position whereby he is resting upright on the knees. He then sits back in such a manner that the buttocks rest on the heels. The toes should be extended to the rear. The trunk is then inclined slightly backward with the hands resting lightly on the ground beside the hips.

Exercise: On command, the trunk is inclined as far backward as it can go until the upper back touches the ground. The hands may be utilized if needed to alleviate undue pain in the legs. The extreme position should be held for a period of six to ten seconds and then repeated twice.

145

GROUP III.   This exercise is designed to stretch the flexor muscles of the shoulder joint.   These may be described as those muscles that cross the front of the shoulder joint.

Figure 1

Figure 2

Exercise 3.   Elbow Toucher.

Arrangement: Students exercise in pairs.

Starting Position: One student lies prone on the ground with the arms moving from a rear position to extend vertically upward.   The standing partner assumes a straddle-squat position over the prone partner and grasps the elbows from the outside.

Exercise: On command, the upper partner presses the elbows in toward each other as far as possible.   This position is held for six to ten seconds and repeated twice.   Partners then exchange positions and repeat the exercise.

146

GROUP IV.   This exercise is designed to stretch the depressor muscles of the humerus.   These may be described as those muscles that cross underneath the shoulder joint.

Figure 1

Figure 2

Exercise 4.   Arm Pusher.

    Arrangement: Students exercise in pairs.

    Starting Position: One student lies prone on the ground with the arms moving from a rear position to extend vertically upward.   The standing partner assumes a straddle-squat position over the prone partner and grasps the elbows from the outside.

    Exercise: On command, the upper partner pushes the prone partner's arms forward as far as possible.   This position is held for six to ten seconds and repeated twice.   Partners then exchange positions and repeat the exercise.

GROUP V.   This exercise is designed to stretch the hamstring group of muscles located behind the thigh and knee joint.

Figure 1

Figure 2

Exercise 5.   Hamstring Stretcher.

Arrangement: Students exercise in pairs.

Starting Position: One student sits on the ground with legs straight and spread wide apart.   The trunk leans forward as far as possible with the arms stretched forward on the ground.   The partner straddles and rests his hands on the sitting partner's back.

Exercise: On command, the standing partner presses down on the sitting partner's back, forcing the chest toward the ground.   This position is held for six to ten seconds and repeated twice.   The partners exchange positions and repeat the exercise.

GROUP VI.   This exercise is designed for extending the upper part of the trunk. Many muscles of the back will be forced to work in this position and a stretch put on the abdominal muscles.

Figure 1

Figure 2

Exercise 6.   Back Extender.

Arrangement: Students exercise in pairs.

Starting Position: The exercising partner gets into a kneeling position on both knees, arms across the chest, with trunk inclined backward. His partner straddles the hips and leaning forward places his hands under the kneeling partner's back and just above the hips.

Exercise: On command, the kneeling partner inclines the trunk as far backward and downward as possible, as the standing partner offers support with his hands. This position is held for six to ten seconds and repeated twice. Partners exchange positions and repeat the exercise.

GROUP VII.   This exercise is designed to exercise the adductor group of muscles located on the inside of the upper legs.

Figure 1

Figure 2

Exercise 7.   Lateral Leg Split.

Arrangement: Students exercise in individual alignment.

Starting Position: From a standing position, the student moves the legs apart laterally as far as possible allowing the crotch to near the ground. A hand may be placed on either side of the crotch for support, if needed.

Exercise: On command, the student gently forces the feet wider apart attempting to lower the crotch to touch the ground. The hands may help to support the body weight to avoid excessive pain. This position is held for six to ten seconds and repeated twice.

GROUP VIII. This exercise is designed to stretch the flexor group of muscles of one thigh, and the extensor group of muscles of the opposite thigh. For this reason, when repeat exercises are done, the position of the legs should be reversed.

Figure 1

Figure 2

Exercise 8.   Fore-Aft Leg Split.

Arrangement: Students exercise in individual alignment.

Starting Position: The student stretches one leg straight forward as the other one is stretched straight to the rear, with both knees kept straight. One hand may be placed on the ground on either side of the body.

Exercise: On command, the student gently separates the feet, lowering the crotch as far as possible toward the ground. The hands may be used to support the body weight to prevent excessive pain, if needed. This position is held for six to ten seconds and repeated twice.

E.   GENERAL CONDITIONING EXERCISES

From the preceding categories of exercises, it is readily seen that many identical exercises can be used in a different approach to achieve a variety of results, ranging from strength to flexibility.

When a coach or physical education instructor gives a series of so-called "conditioning" exercises on the field or in the class, such exercises many times do not achieve true and progressive conditioning. The term "conditioning" normally implies improvement when applied to physical exercise. The way such exercises are normally conducted, however, they act only as maintenance of the present status of physical capability of the body.

In order to improve significantly the physical condition of a person's body, the work load must be gradually increased - as has been suggested in an earlier discussion in this text. Consequently, as the exercises are given daily, over a period of days, each exercise should have an increase in repetitions while the time given to execute the exercise is held constant; or, the repetitions of each exercise should be held constant with a gradual decrease in the time allowed to execute the exercise. In either instance the rate of movement, or rate of performing work, has been brought about and constitutes progressive resistance.

A number of the exercises already mentioned previously may be used to form a general set of conditioning exercises. The instructor may be more familiar with a set of exercises of his own design which he may prefer to use. The point is that movements involving use of large muscles of the body - in any pattern - may be subjected to the conditioning formula. When so used, one might expect a more rapid rate of improvement in the ability of the body to perform work and hence improve the physical condition of the person.

Much has been written concerning the proper way to design a set of calisthenic exercises. The exercises would be designed in such manner that major muscle groups would be required to work vigorously. Sometimes a pattern of covering the muscle groups of the body would be suggested. Attention would be given to so arrange the series of exercises that no one group of muscles would be worked hard twice in succession. The FM 21-20 Physical Training Manual designed for use by the War Department[1] during World War II has such exercises illustrated. Staley[2] has written a book that deals specifically with exercise programs.

In physical conditioning an objective may be to improve one's "wind", or to improve his ability to do vigorous, sustained exercise without incurring a severe oxygen debt. An example would be to run a mile in four minutes or less. In approaching this objective, running at controlled pace times, or employing the interval training technique, would be much preferred to calisthenic exercises.

When running is not feasible, however, the set of exercises given earlier that pertain to muscular endurance may be utilized. One may note, in the performance of this set, that increased respiration results from the vigorous activity. Even so, an exercise of running vigorously in place might well be added to the set.

---

[1]
War Department, Physical Training, FM 21-20. War Department Field Manual, Washington, D. C., 1946.

[2]
Staley, Charles S., Physical Exercise Programs, The C. V. Mosby Company, St. Louis, Missouri, 1953.

NOTES:

CHAPTER   I V.

COMMENTARY ON RELATED ACTIVITIES

This chapter contains forty-nine outlines for

three minute talks on a wide variety of sub-

jects related to physical education and good

health practices in general.

****

The COMMENTARY ON RELATED ACTIVITIES should last from three to five minutes. At times the talk will concern the things to be done during the class period. However, sometimes the same activity is repeated for several days; then if the period is to be a learning session there are many other things which should be brought to the attention of the student during his stay in school. It is sufficient if they are related to the great general field covering physical well-being and developing emotionally.

It is merely the purpose of the following items to give the instructor a broad general outline. He is to feel what is necessary and fill in the gaps. If he is not familiar with the subject, then it would be better if he avoid it. The following should give the physical educator many ideas:

Falling Out of Boats

how to shed clothing .. remove shoes first .. hold on to boat .. hold anything that would aid flotation .. U.S.C.G. recommendations when followed, would avoid many unpleasant incidents.

Burns

explain the meaning of degrees in burns .. uses of medicines .. avoiding scars .. flashfires .. extinguishers to avoid.

Tournaments

single elimination .. consolation .. double elimination .. fastest method of determining a champion .. advantages and reasons for use of each kind.

Byes in Tournaments

to find the number of byes, take the number of entries and subtract it from the next perfect multiple of four .. hence, when a champion is determined from a group of eleven, the number of byes is five, because sixteen is the next highest multiple of four .. if there were seventeen entries from which a champion was to be determined, then, it would be fifteen byes, because the next perfect multiple of four is thirty-two.

League Play

Mathematics .. N (N-1) is used for a single round robin .. double round robin system .. methods of arriving at playing schedule.

Ecchymosis

to prevent, duck in time .. apply cold compresses immediately for fifteen minutes .. internal damage might be indicated .. in case it does, consult a physician .. validity of homemade remedies.

Badminton

history .. method of scoring .. care and cost of equipment .. value as a backyard sport .. court dimensions.

The Lariat

its use in the early West .. type of rope needed .. use for exhibition purposes .. practical uses on farms.

Shuffle Board

history .. method of scoring .. value for the older people .. care and cost of equipment .. court dimensions.

Fly Tying

why fish strike .. imitating the insect .. equipment needed .. value as a home hobby .. business possibilities .. cost of beginners kit.

The Common Cold

where it comes from .. its prevention .. its control .. its treatment .. fallacies.

Fly Fishing

Isaac Walton .. the purists .. sources for buying rods and reels .. value for outdoor living and as a lifelong sport.

Fishing Accidents

removing fish hooks from flesh .. cutting off the hook .. first aid after the field surgery .. snake bite.

Broken Limbs

how to handle .. in the field splinting .. keeping the patient comfortable and calm .. bleeding .. the pressure points .. compress bandages .. keeping wound closed .. methods and dangers of lacing bleeding wounds too tightly.

Hair Cuts

short cropped hair dries easier .. social acceptance of exaggerated male hair styles .. value of tonics.

Pros and Cons of Hair Tonics

values of oils and creams on the scalp .. effect of alcohol in tonics .. water on the hair .. baldness causes .. fallacies.

Weight Lifting

usually a series of exercises performed with a small percentage of ones weight .. danger of lifting without instruction .. hazard of "seeing how much you can lift" .. danger of working out alone.

Value of the Team

higher quality of competition and proficiency needed .. satisfies urge to work with others toward a common goal .. recognition in acceptable areas .. educational value.

History of Basketball

first played in Springfield, Massachusetts .. Dr. James Naismith inventor .. describe the early game and first rules .. local history of the sport .. present status.

Tennis

early history in Europe .. Early history in the United States .. Davis Cup play .. the scoring .. cost of equipment and the court.

Track Meet Cautions

discus flight unpredictable .. participants and spectators both in the danger zones when close to the thrower .. same cautions for the shotput.

Handling a Gun

treat every gun as a loaded gun .. keep loaded guns out of camp, car, boat .. be sure barrel is free from obstructions .. carry gun so that muzzle direction is away from partner .. do not point the gun at anything not to be shot at .. never leave unattended a loaded gun.

Carrying a Gun

cross a fence by putting the gun through the fence first, then crawl through after the gun .. be sure of target and what is behind the target .. do not shoot at water, ice, or hard surfaces, it could cause bullet skidding.

Strange Stream Swimming

inspect areas for obstacles first before diving .. beware of sharp roots or broken glass .. avoid swimming down stream from pollution sources .. private lands require permission to avoid trespassing.

Hunting Safety

wear distinctive colors .. orange, yellow, or red .. too much clothing is as bad as not enough .. clothing for warmth should not be too tight .. good fitting boots mean warm feet and less fatigue.

Hunting Manners

get land owner's permission .. use care crossing fences ..
close gates .. hunt away from livestock .. thank land owner
at the end of hunt.

Hunting Rules

get state license .. observe bad limits .. have license available for inspection .. hunt only in season .. use proper
weapon.

Callouses on the Feet

use proper fitting shoes .. keep them soft .. keep callouses
thin to avoid blisters underneath them .. home surgery is
very dangerous.

How to Take a Bath

keep the hair dry .. watch for scalding water .. wipe off
excess water with the hand before using the towel .. dry from
top down .. get between the toes.

Locker Room Conduct

practical jokes are dangerous .. shower floors are slippery
.. help keep the locker room clean by not discarding material
on the floors .. use the containers provided .. respect
locker rights of other individuals.

Falls on Cinders

wash thoroughly with soap and water .. flush away as much
foreign material as possible .. get first aid .. necessity
for probable tetanus shot .. treat daily .. use ointment dressing when indicated.

Spike Wounds and Punctures

allow to bleed .. wash away possible foreign particles .. keep
wound open .. refer to physician.

Hair and the Shower

avoid getting hair wet unless the intent is to actually wash it ..
daily washing is not always recommended .. the shower cap.

Poison Ivy

recognition of the plant .. superstitions for cures .. home
remedies and others .. other poison plants.

Insect Bites

use of repellents .. mechanical guards .. recognition of the
insect to indicate the treatment necessary.

The Olympics

its history .. methods of qualifying .. recent experience
in the Olympics .. prominent persons .. records .. try to
tie in with physical education activities

Boy Scouts

its origin and purpose .. history .. method of organization ..
merit badge motivation.

Mountain Climbing

why it is done .. equipment .. dangers and rewards .. costs
prominent names and places.

German Gymnastics

19th century history .. history in this country .. its contribu-
tion to modern physical education .. Turner Halls.

Water Safety

swimming in protected areas .. indirect accidents resulting
from swimming .. danger of diving and ducking other people
.. related hazards.

Artificial Respiration

mouth to mouth .. others .. accepted principals of giving artificial respiration .. how to assist.

Dealing with Cramps

in the water .. other places .. how to massage .. how to avoid .. probable reasons.

Physical Education Class Procedure

receiving and exchanging towels .. disposition of worn out clothing .. opening and closing time .. fees $ .. help cut utility bills by turning off lights and shutting off the water.

Gym Shoes

keep shoes clean inside and out .. powder frequently .. no rawhide, cloth laces only .. replace knotted laces .. lace the entire shoe .. use the proper shoe to match the activity .. danger of ill-fitting footwear.

Gym Clothing

be sure that it is clean .. change frequently .. have personal clothing identified with indelible ink .. wear appropriate clothing for the activity .. be sure that it fits properly .. uniform style is best.

Care of the Feet

dry thoroughly after the shower to avoid fungus diseases .. athletes foot can be prevented or cured by using proper treatment .. explain uses of foot tubs and powder boxes .. suspicions of the fungus should be reported.

Foot Blisters

do not open .. sanitation is necessary .. avoid by wearing proper fitting shoes and getting feet in condition gradually.

Specks in the Eye

do not rub as it may lodge the foreign body .. lift upper eye-
lid over the lower lid and let tears wash out the offending
particle .. keep eye closed with light dressing .. danger of
layman in probing.

Physical Education as a Career

education needed to qualify as an instructor .. courses covered in college .. schools in the area offering training ..
costs of this type of education .. length of time required ..
advantages and disadvantages of physical education as a
career.

CHAPTER   V.

SMALL   AREA   GAMES

****

SMALL AREA GAMES

Duck - on - the - rock

A paper box or stool is designated as the goal. A throwing line is drawn about twenty feet away. A piece of soft rubber or other harmless object, such as a blackboard eraser, is given to each player. To decide who is IT all stand on the throwing line and toss their rocks at the goal. The one landing the greatest distance away is IT. IT places his rock on the goal, and stands near to guard it. The others in turn try to throw and knock the duck off. When it is knocked off, all who have thrown run to pick up their rocks and return to the line. IT may tag them as soon as he replaces his duck on the box. Players who fail to knock the duck off may run to get their rocks at any time, but are liable to capture. The first one tagged is IT. Then, the sequence repeats itself.

Dead Man

A group of ten or twelve sit on the floor, feet to the center. In this center a designated boy stands stiff, hands at side, and falls in any direction. He is passed around the circle by the sitters. The one who fails to pass him on is the next Dead Man.

Pull Across the Line

Draw a line thirty or forty feet long. Place one half of the group on one side and the other half on the other side of the line. The object is to pull any of the opposition over. Any part of the body is a pullover and the use of two on one is fair play. Those who have been pulled over are out of play. This is best played on a time basis.

Water Bucket Relay

This is best played out-of-doors where water spilling will not be a problem. Materials, two cups, two buckets, and two milk bottles. This is a passing relay. Place a bucket of water at the head of each line. The first boy dips out a cup and passes the cup down the line to the last boy who pours what water remains into the bottle. The empty cup must be passed back. The winner is the first to get the bottle full.

167

Swat the Fly

This is a circle game for twenty-five or less. The swatter is made of heavy denim with cotton two inches thick and about sixteen inches long. All face the inside of the circle, hands behind their backs ready to receive the swatter. The game starts with the instructor running around the back of the circle and placing the swatter in a boy's hand. This boy is now the swatter and immediately starts beating the boy on his right on the buttocks. The boy being swatted has to run all the way around the circle to escape being hit and return to his original position. The boy being swatted becomes the next swatter. Boys who peek must go to the center of the circle, place hands on knees and get a free swat. CAUTION: Hit only the buttocks.

Balloon Volleyball

An ordinary toy balloon is used. A rope about seven feet high may serve as a net. Establish sidelines, only. A serving line might be two paces from the net, depending upon the weight of the balloon. The balloon may be relayed any number of times, provided no player bats it twice in succession.

Crawl the Chair

Place a clean cloth on the seat of a chair with a part of it hanging over the right edge. Sit down with legs over the right edge, then, grasp the back of the chair and with head and shoulders in advance, creep around the chair and reach the cloth and retrieve, using the teeth. Any part of the body touching the floor disqualifies.

One Foot Squat

Stand on one foot and extend the other foot in front. Dip to a full squat position with the arms out at the side and return to a standing position without touching any other part of the body, the floor, or losing balance.

Sit Through

Extend the body to a position where the body is suspended between the hands and the toes. Then, by placing the body in tuck position jump through the arms and end in sitting position.

Black Eye

Use a leather volleyball deflated about one-fourth.

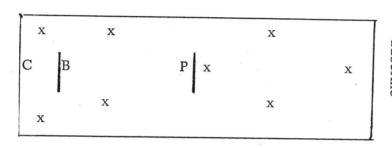

B B B B B B B B B B B

Bs are at bat. B stands on free throw line with his back toward the pitcher. Other Bs sit in batting order on the sideline. The team in the field scatter any place, except that in the front court, not over four men, in addition to the Pitcher and the Catcher, may be there, and none may be closer to the batter than four steps.

To start the game the Pitcher throws at the Batter underhanded. Three throws are allowed. Batter is probably crouched, so the target is the buttocks. If the Pitcher misses all three times, the batter goes to the far end to the Baseline. If he hits the batter, even slightly, the batter runs for the baseline. He may be tagged out only by being hit by a thrown ball. The tag must be made by a two-hand throw.

As many may be on the far baseline at one time as can reach it. No lead off is allowed, and if the runner leaves he may be played on. A run is scored by return to the Homebase line, which is the opposite wall at any point. All may run at the same time, or the return may be staggered.

Other rules: If the batter in position "flinches" when the ball is pitched, he is out. Path of runners may not be impeded. Floor bounce pitches are walks. An inning is three outs.

NOTES:

CHAPTER VI.

INTRODUCTORY ROUTINES FOR SPORT ACTIVITIES

Trampoline Routines

Introductory Tumbling Routines

Tumbling, Doubles and Triples

Tennis Routines, with Bankboard

Tennis Routines, Courts

Weight Lifting Routines

Rope Skipping Routines

Basketball Routines

TRAMPOLINE ROUTINES

1. ## Seat to Stand

   All spot, surround trampoline completely; no somersaults permitted. Land on the center of canvas, legs straight, hands parallel to buttocks with fingers pointed forward. Work with the spring of the canvas.

2. ## Knees to Stand

   Back straight, keep the head up, land on knees and the instep of feet. Use arms in rhythm for getting lift.

3. ## Knees to Seat

   From knee position throw legs through to seat and back to a stand.

4. ## Knees one half twist to Knees

   Head up, back straight, use spring of canvas, head turned with shoulders in the direction of body spin. Back to feet.

5. ## Bound and Tuck

   Bound up and while up draw knees to chest and grasp shins with the hands.

6. ## Standing Full Turn

   Begin turn near the top of spring, turning head and shoulders together in direction of turn. Maintain balance.

7. ## Standing, Full Twist to Knees

   Back straight, head up, turn at top of spring and land on knees and instep. Back to feet.

8. ## Seat One Half Twist to Seat

   Get height, use force of trampoline and spring of push with hands.

9. Back to Feet

   Keep looking at the framework at the far end of trampoline
   as long as possible, head on chest. Do not allow feet to get
   over head. Be certain to land on the back, not buttocks or
   neck.

10. Seat to Belly

    Knees stiff, fingers pointing forward, hands used on mat
    and placed parallel to buttocks. Push from seat to stomach
    to feet.

11. Back to Belly

    From position No. 9 push off mat, swing with legs tucked under
    body, and come to seat. Then to feet.

12. Forward Somersault

    The instructor must decide when the performer is ready for
    this stunt.

13. Back Somersault

    The instructor must decide when the performer is ready for
    this stunt.

    The instructor should proceed from the simple to the difficult.
    Add below such supplementary routines as would seem necessary to
    create an orderly routine. Insist on no unsupervised use of the
    trampoline.

INTRODUCTORY TUMBLING ROUTINES

1. Forward roll use hands .. tuck.

2. Forward roll use hands, go off of right foot, then repeat off of the left foot.

3. Forward roll with arms folded.

4. Forward roll with arms extended at side, then from each foot.

5. Forward roll with legs crossed, hold toes.

6. Backward roll, place hands near ears.

7. Backward roll, with extension to stand up.

8. Backward roll, from stiff leg stand.

9. Balance with knees on elbows.

10. Headstand from knee balance. Head and hands make triangle. If the balance of the body is lost when in upright position, tuck and roll out.

11. Head stand arms folded.

12. Head stand using forearms.

13. Hand stand from knee and elbow balance .. spot.

14. Hand stand against the wall.

15. From a hand stand, walk on hands.

16. Dive from standing position .. gradually increase height and distance.

17. Dive over objects .. keep safe reserve distance.

18. Cartwheel.

19. Handspring .. use rolled up mat .. double the mat for landing.

20. Back handspring .. this is advanced .. do not try until free backbend can be done easily .. use lunge belt.

21. Front running somersault .. use rolled mat, double the landing mat.

22. Back somersault .. use lunge belt.

TUMBLING .. DOUBLES AND TRIPLES

1. Thigh stand from a crotch lift .. spot all.

2. Thigh stand from a back pullover.

3. Knee stand.

4. Shoulder stand on thighs.

5. Double roll forward with partner.

6. Back roll with partner.

7. Two big boys swing one light boy, hands and feet, to up position with face down. ONE should be under 100#.

8. Two big boys swing one, face up, left hand, left foot, right hand, right foot, to up position.

9. Two swing one to a catcher. Catcher stands close and gradually increases the distance.

10. Two make one as a swinging rope.

11. Stand on shoulders using two or three different mounts.

12. Hand to foot balance .. do on mat.

13. Head stand on back. spot.

14. Shoulder stand on thighs.

15. Shuffle roll with three boys.

16. Triple thigh stand. spot.

17. Handspring on knees with an assist from bottom man.

18. Bottom man uses feet to balance top man as a human barrel.

19.   Multiple horse walk.

20.   Skin the Snake.

21.   Two boys do thigh and toe neck hook on big bottom man.

22.   Arm to Arm balance on bottom man. spot.

23.   Shoulder stand on feet of bottom man. spot.

The progression must be orderly, go from the simple to the difficult. Nothing must be performed until it is thoroughly mastered. While some of the above items have spot indications, everything should be spotted. The spotters must be trained to think defensively.

TENNIS ROUTINES .. (Use bankboard)

1. Forehand to wall. Drop the ball and step into it for a full stroke. Work for five to ten consecutive strokes in good form.

2. Back hand to wall. Drop ball and step into it. Work for five to ten consecutive strokes in good form.

3. Alternate forehand and backhand. Work for ten to twenty consecutive strokes in good form.

4. Serve to wall and return with ten forehands .. then ten backhands .. then alternate.

5. Work with a partner. Partner serves to the wall, and boys alternately return the ball to the wall until one misses. Winner serves the next series.

6. Partner tosses ball high, and the ball is smashed to the wall.

TENNIS ROUTINES .. (On courts)

1. Five minutes volley from base line.

2. Five minutes volley by north side with south up at net.

3. Five minutes volley by south side with north up at net.

4. Five minutes service by south, north merely blocks ball.

5. Five minutes service by north, south merely blocks ball.

6. Five minutes lobbing by north, south smashes.

7. Five minutes lobbing by south, north smashes.

8. Five minutes returning service to designated spot by north.

9. Five minutes returning service to designated spot by south.

All periods should be concluded with at least some competitive play. Encourage the use of a bankboard to improve form.

It is good motivation to arrange boys in an order of probable ability, particularly the first ten to fifteen. A boy raises his rank by beating the boy above him in rank, or any boy above him. For example: No. 7 beats No. 3. No. 7 then becomes No. 6 even though he has not played him. It is wise to allow ranks to change frequently. This can be arranged by allowing the winner of just one set to rise in rank. [1]

---

[1]Griffin, J.H., "A Tennis Program for Small Schools," Scholastic Coach, 33:50-52, April, 1964.

WEIGHT LIFTING ROUTINES

1. Progression
   a. Use bar that has about thirty per cent of body weight. (If a person weighs 150 pounds, then forty-five pounds is plenty.)
   b. The first sessions do all recommended exercises four to six times and every other day increase the number of times until it reaches from thirteen to fifteen.
   c. Add five pounds and repeat the progression as above.
   d. Add weights as long as it seems reasonable. Three to five rounds of weight increasing would seem like a good introduction to weight training.

2. Basic exercises
   a. Raise bar from the floor to the waist, to shoulder, to overhead. Bring back to the floor in the same three motions.
   b. From shoulder position press bar overhead.
   c. Place bar on the back of shoulders and rise on toes. (Boys with bad arches should check on this series with the coach.)
   d. Bar on shoulders, deep knee bends.
   e. Lie on floor, with stiff arm pull bar from back of head to upright position. Reduce weight for this exercise.
   f. Stiff legs, lift bar to belly.
   g. Curl. With bar at waist raise the bar to the shoulder with a curling motion.
   h. Straddle lift. Lift bar from floor to crotch.
   i. Bar on shoulders. Twist to far right, then to far left.
   j. Two hand press from prone position. This is dangerous, have a spotter.
   k. Shrug. Add weight. Bring bar to waist, then with shoulders only and stiff arms, raise bar four to six inches.
   l. There are other competitive events that can be added, but the above are sufficient for an introduction.

3. Cautions
   a. Do not allow this to be a weight lifting contest.
   b. Do not allow unsupervised work with weights.
   c. See that weights are fixed securely to the bar.
   d. Get the weight off the floor with the use of leg muscles, not the back.

e. Three or four boys to a bar is plenty. This will make good use of the bar in an ordinary physical education period.

f. For motivation take body measurements before and after each major series of exercises. It is good to give a day of rest between each weight training session. A unit of rope skipping run concurrently with the weight lifting is a good loosening up activity and variation from what could be a dull routine.

ROPE SKIPPING ROUTINES

1. Turn rope forward and jump on right foot.

2. Turn rope forward and jump on left foot.

3. Turn rope forward and jump with both feet.

4. Turn rope forward and alternate left foot and right foot.

5. Turn rope forward and jump two times on right foot, then

6. Turn rope forward and jump two times on left foot, then

7. Turn rope forward and continue the two foot continuity.

8. Turn rope forward and cross right hand over left for all of the above, and

9. Turn rope forward and cross left hand over right for all of the above.

10. Turn rope back for right foot.

11. Turn rope back for left foot.

12. Turn rope back for both feet.

13. Turn rope forward and do combinations of the above.

14. Turn rope backward and do combinations of the above.

15. Turn rope for all of the above, but use stiff forward knee action.

16. Turn rope for all of the above, but use high knee action.

17. Turn rope twice for all of the above, but start on easily mastered turns.

18. Turn rope and vary routines .. with spread legs .. clicking heels.

19.   Turn rope and include a facing partner.

20.   Turn rope with partner at side and have partner hold the end of rope on his side.

21.   Turn rope with partner presenting his back.

22.   Turn rope with partner at side .. inside arm on neck .. waist .. arms locked .. holding hands.

ROPE CLIMBING ROUTINES

Going up.

1. Grasp rope high with both hands.

2. Bend right leg in front of body so that the rope hangs against the inside of knee and outside of foot.

3. Raise the left foot from floor, cross the feet.

4. Rope should now be securely clamped between the crossed feet and the knees, body hanging in a sitting position, arms fully extended.

5. Extend knees, raising body from sitting position to upright position. The chest is now level with the hands.

6. Reach and grasp rope as high as possible. Draw the body up on hands, at the same time allowing rope to slide through knees and ankles, arriving as before in a squatting position.

7. Repeat to reach the desired height.

Coming down.

1. Allow the rope to slide between the knees and ankles, lowering the body, hand under hand.

2. Caution, do not allow hands to slide down the rope, this can cause painful burns to hands and inside of thighs.

ROUTINES

1. Climb to the top .. descend without the aid of legs.

2. Climb the rope without the aid of feet.

3. Climb .. legs horizontally forward.

4. Hang with left hand and swing .. hang with right hand.

5. Chin to hands, raising legs horizontally and holding position.

6. Pull up, chinning to hands.

7. Chin to hands, raising legs horizontally, then spread feet wide and hold position.

8. Pull up on arms and touch rope overhead with toes of right foot.

9. Pull up on arms and touch rope over head with toes of left foot.

10. Pull up on arms and touch rope over head with both feet.

11. Pull up on arms and swing legs upward over the shoulder between rope and the body.

12. Pull up, extend legs straight over head and hold the body in a vertical position.

13. Extend body straight upward overhead; twist legs around the rope, hang head down, hold with one hand.

14. Extend body straight upward overhead, twist legs around rope, hang head down, no hands.

15. Interest may be added by having two men on the rope and performing at the same time.

Other items.

1. It is best to use a rope designed for the purpose.

2. Locate ropes where their use will not conflict with other activities.

3. Frequent inspection of rope and fixtures should be made to insure safe conditions.

4. Careful supervision is necessary at all times. Do not work alone.

5. A double mat under the rope provides some protection.

6. Make sure the top attachment is secure and of proper design.

BASKETBALL ROUTINES

1. Right hand lay up. Step forward with the right foot and bounce the ball at the same time, take one step with the left foot, raise the right knee and the ball at the same time. The ball is raised with both hands, but at eye level transfer the ball to the right hand and place the ball against the bankboard about one foot above the rim. (If the coach places his foot lightly on the boy's left foot just before the sequence starts, this is an aid in teaching the boy to get his steps to come out correctly.)

2. For the left hand lay up, use the same technique.

3. Change over dribble. Line up eight or ten boys, each with a ball. Start dribbling in position with the right hand. On signal dribble about twenty feet, keep the ball bouncing, but change hands, then advance another twenty feet. Keep repeating until a round trip up and down the length of the gym is made. This is not a race, but a drill to learn proper form in dribbling.

4. Two hand jump shot. This shot should be practiced at ten feet from the goal with all the emphasis on proper form. Let go of the ball at maximum height and follow through with the fingers. Move back as accuracy and control is gained.

5. Two hand chest shot. Use the same technique as in No. 4. Start close and perfect the form, head up and follow through. As accuracy is gained gradually move back.

6. Dribble, pivot and pass. From the center of the floor drive three or four fast steps .. stop and pivot on the left foot one or two times. (This is assuming that the boy is right handed.) Pass to a trailer boy who times himself for the pass and who after receiving it goes in for the lay up.

7. Dribble, stop, pivot, and shoot. From the center of the floor drive three or four fast steps, stop and pivot on the left foot one or two turns, then rise and shoot. Opposite steps for the left handed boys.

8. Rebounding. For practicing rebounding, toss the ball against the bankboard and the boy rebounds the ball as many times as possible first with the right hand, then with the left hand, then alternate hands, and finally use both hands.

9. Two man rebounding. Boy on both sides of the basket bounce the ball on the board and across to the other side. This is returned a set number of times and when the announced number is reached the ball is placed into the basket.

10. Tandem rebounding. Boys may line up one behind the other and rebound on the board. On signal one of the boys puts the ball in.

11. The four basic offensive fundamentals are shooting, pivoting, dribbling, and passing.

12. Parts of the offensive pattern to be used in actual play make the best drills.

Defensive form is probably best learned by the whole method while the general defensive pattern is being worked as a team. If the defense is straight man for man defense, then it would seem that one on one, one with the ball and trying to get to the basket and the other trying to stop him and actually end up with the ball. This contains all the elements of individual play under competitive conditions. Two on two accomplishes the same purpose, but adds the passing.

CHAPTER VII.

ALL AROUND ATHLETE, POINT SYSTEM, JUNIOR
AND ADVANCED

ALMOST AN ALL AROUND ATHLETE

****

ALL AROUND ATHLETE   .. A. A. A.

Physical education classes can be motivated by setting up standards that should be attainable by average boys. These events may be set up to cover many of the activities involved in major sports, and activities demanding skills that can only be achieved through training and self-discipline.

To qualify as an ALL AROUND ATHLETE or an ALMOST AN ALL AROUND ATHLETE, the completion of from twelve to sixteen events should be required in four years of school. In order to maintain interest throughout the student's stay in school, it might be well not to require that the events be completed at any particular time or in any specific year. As a matter of fact they might be done during the vacations or after the student has completed his school work, if his interests continue. All that would be necessary would be that the events be performed in the presence of a reliable person, such as Y. M. C. A. instructors, any of the coaching staff, or even a committee of boys who have already completed all of the requirements.

Recognition in the form of certificates for each event completed, an inexpensive medal for the completion of all of the requirements, plus the mounting of the name on a board or plaque in a prominent place in the school further adds to the interest. Few activities academic or otherwise succeed without promotion. Students want and need recognition. It is good if the physical education program can provide wholesome situations for young adults in which to excel.

The standards for the ALL AROUND ATHLETE are sufficiently high to demand maximum effort in many cases. The local situation will determine the number and the type of events. There should be some events that almost all could complete. Perfect attendance for a year gives a boy four opportunities to gain a point by merely being present. The B average gives the uncoordinated boy another chance to gain a point if he has classroom skill. Being on a winning team or winning some group activity during the four year stay will usually allow some boy to earn a point, some times by merely being associated with a good group.

ALL AROUND ATHLETE .. Events

	Events	Requirements
1.	100 yards	12 seconds
2.	440 yards	60 seconds
3.	880 yards	2:45 minutes
4.	Mile	6 minutes
5.	Broad jump	17 feet
6.	High jump	5 feet
7.	Baseball throw	250 feet
8.	100 yard swim	2 minutes
9.	Handstand or Headstand	10 seconds
10.	Rope Twirling	60 seconds
11.	Rope skipping (cross hands left and right once)	150 times
12.	Free throws	25 of 28 tries
13.	Perfect attendance for	1 year
14.	Chin ups on a horizontal bar	13 times
15.	Push ups	25 times
16.	Belly stretchers	25 times
17.	Scholastic grades .. B average	1 year
18.	Earn a major letter once	Any year or sport
19.	Put SHOT .. 12 pounds	33 feet
20.	Juggle three objects	1 minute

21.	Play 9 holes of golf in not over 9 over par	
22.	Jump the loop formed by holding the foot with hand	once
23.	Earn a minor letter in two varsity sports	
24.	Hand spring	once
25.	Pullover on a horizontal bar	once
26.	Belly stretchers	25 times

ALMOST AN ALL AROUND ATHLETE [1] .. Events .. Requirements

	Events	Requirements
1.	100 yards	13 seconds
2.	440 yards	65 seconds
3.	880 yards	3 minutes
4.	Mile	7 minutes
5.	Broad jump	15 feet
6.	High jump	4 - 6
7.	Baseball throw	200 feet
8.	100 yard swim	2 1/2 minutes
9.	Hand stand or Head stand	30 seconds
10.	Rope twirling	30 seconds
11.	Rope skipping (cross hands left and right once)	100 times

---

[1]Griffin, J.H., "All Around Athlete Tests and Standards," Scholastic Coach, 24:54 - 55, November, 1954.

12.	Perfect attendance for	1 year
13.	Average scholastic grades B for	1 year
14.	Chin ups on a horizontal bar	10 times
15.	Push ups	20 times
16.	Belly stretchers	20 times
17.	Earn a minor letter	1 time
18.	Hand spring	1 time
19.	Put 12 pound shot	30 feet
20.	Jump the loop formed by holding the foot with hand	1 time
21.	Be on a winning team in a tourney, or win a tourney	1 time
22.	Play 9 holes of golf in not over 9 over par	
23.	Pullover on a horizontal bar	1 time
24.	Juggle three objects	1 minute
25.	Earn a major letter	1 time

It will be noted that the same group of events is used for the lower teenage boy, but the requirements for qualification are considerably lowered. Some form of recognition should be given, the following is a form which could be used for recognition of the completion of any of the required events:

All Around Athlete

_____ has met the

requirements for _____

His record was _____

The minimum requirement is _____

Date_____   Approved by_____

Community High School   Title_____

NOTES:

CHAPTER VIII.

CHARTS FOR TOURNAMENTS AND LEAGUE PLAY

League and Tournament Play

Double Elimination Tournament

****

LEAGUE PLAY AND TOURNAMENT PLAY

Physical education activities may be motivated in many cases with league play and tournaments. A single elimination tournament is the fastest way to determine a champion. With league play, however, it is possible for all teams entered in an activity to play against every other team. There are many variations of tournament play, and these may follow patterns where losers have an opportunity to gain a championship by way of a two-way bracket. Three basic tournament forms are illustrated.

Bye

  A

   A

B

    A

C

  B

D

     A

  D

E

    D

Bye

  F

F

     G

     Champion...

Bye

  G

G

    G

H

     Third place

  H

I

     D

    G   D

J

     J

  J

K

    J

L

  L

M

There are always the same number of contests in a tourney as the number entered, less one. The exception is when there is a third place playoff as in the preceding tournament. There are always the same number of byes as the number of teams entered less the next perfect multiple of four. Hence, in the preceding tournament there are three byes. Note: Thirteen teams entered plus three byes equals sixteen.

The losers in the first round may play off as the following illustrates the preceding tournament for thirteen:

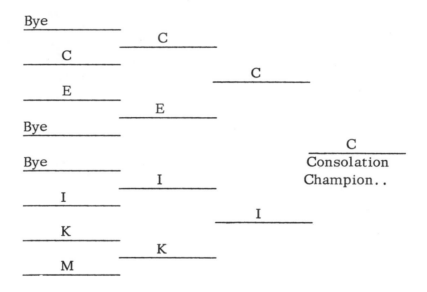

Double Elimination Tournament

The right half of a double elimination tournament proceeds as any other tourney for the winners, but it is so arranged that two defeats are necessary before elimination. It is also possible for the winner of the left half of the bracket to eventually meet the right half champion and have a playoff. League play is usually more desirable, but for purposes of illustration the loser's bracket is drawn on the next page. Note the comments which will be at the bottom of the bracket filled in with theoretical winners and losers.

16 Team <u>Double</u> <u>Elimination</u> <u>Tournament</u> .. championship bracket

A
    A
B
        A
C
    D
D
            A
E
    E
F
        E
G
    G
H

               A
               Winner of champion-
               ship bracket

I
    I
J
        I
K
    K
L
            I
M
    M
N
        M
O
    O
P

The loser's bracket is on the next page drawn up based upon the winners and losers as indicated in this championship bracket illustration. A will meet the winner of the left half of the bracket. The procedure for this will be discussed following the loser's diagram.

DOUBLE ELIMINATION TOURNAMENT

Loser's bracket (left side)

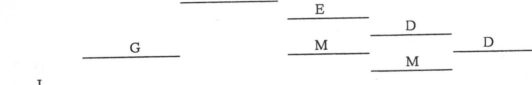

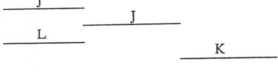

```
  B
      B
  C
            D

      D
  F
      F
  H
            G
                E
                    D
      G           M       D
                        M
  J
      J
  L
            K

      K
                    K
  N
      N
  P
            O

      O
```

Based upon the above D has only one defeat, hence must play A. If D wins then each has had but one defeat, so to carry the tournament to its logical conclusion one more contest should be played with the winner to be either A or D.

League play offers the greatest opportunity for the most play. The formula for determining the number of contests in a series in which each team plays every other team once is:

$$\frac{N(N-1)}{2} \quad \text{N equals the number of entrants}$$

This is a single round robin. A double round robin results merely by applying the following: $N(N-1)$. Of course, the series may be repeated as many times as is desired.

The following are some examples of the single round robin:

4 Team Schedule

```
1 - 4    1 - 2    1 - 3
2 - 3    3 - 4    4 - 2
```

5 Team Schedule

```
1 - 4    2 - 5    3 - 1    4 - 2    5 - 3
2 - 3    3 - 4    4 - 5    5 - 1    1 - 2
```

6 Team Schedule

```
1 - 6    1 - 2    1 - 3    1 - 4    1 - 5
2 - 5    3 - 6    4 - 2    5 - 3    6 - 4
3 - 4    4 - 5    5 - 6    6 - 2    2 - 3
```

7   Team Schedule

```
1 - 6   2 - 5   3 - 4   2 - 7   3 - 6   4 - 5   3 - 1
4 - 7   5 - 6   4 - 2   5 - 1   6 - 7   5 - 3   6 - 2
7 - 1   6 - 4   7 - 3   1 - 2   7 - 5   1 - 4   2 - 3
```

8   Team Schedule

```
1 - 8   2 - 7   3 - 6   4 - 5   1 - 2   3 - 8   4 - 7
5 - 6   1 - 3   4 - 2   5 - 8   6 - 7   1 - 4   5 - 3
6 - 2   7 - 8   1 - 5   6 - 4   7 - 3   8 - 2   1 - 6
7 - 5   8 - 4   2 - 3   1 - 7   8 - 6   2 - 5   3 - 4
```

9   Team Schedule

```
1 - 8   2 - 7   3 - 6   4 - 5   1 - 9   3 - 8   4 - 7
5 - 6   1 - 2   4 - 9   5 - 8   6 - 7   1 - 3   5 - 2
6 - 9   7 - 8   1 - 4   6 - 3   7 - 2   8 - 9   1 - 5
7 - 4   8 - 3   9 - 2   1 - 6   8 - 5   9 - 4   2 - 3
1 - 7   9 - 6   2 - 5   3 - 4   2 - 9   3 - 8   4 - 7
                                                5 - 6
```

10   Team Schedule

```
1 - 10   2 - 9   3 - 8   4 - 7   5 - 6   1 - 2   3 - 10
4 - 9    5 - 8   6 - 7   1 - 2   4 - 1   5 - 10  6 - 9
7 - 8    1 - 3   5 - 2   6 - 1   7 - 10  8 - 9   1 - 4
6 - 3    7 - 2   8 - 1   9 - 10  1 - 6   7 - 5   8 - 4
9 - 3    10 - 2  1 - 7   8 - 6   9 - 5   10 - 4  2 - 3
1 - 8    9 - 7   10 - 6  1 - 5   3 - 4   1 - 9   10 - 8
2 - 7    3 - 6   4 - 5
```

11 Team Schedule

1 - 10	2 - 9	3 - 8	4 - 7	5 - 6	1 - 11	3 - 10
4 - 9	5 - 8	6 - 7	1 - 2	4 - 11	5 - 10	6 - 9
7 - 8	1 - 2	4 - 11	5 - 10	6 - 9	7 - 8	1 - 3
5 - 2	6 - 11	7 - 10	9 - 9	1 - 4	6 - 3	7 - 2
8 - 11	9 - 10	1 - 5	7 - 4	8 - 3	9 - 2	10 - 11
1 - 6	8 - 5	9 - 4	10 - 3	11 - 2	1 - 5	9 - 4
10 - 3	11 - 2	1 - 8	10 - 7	11 - 6	2 - 5	3 - 4
1 - 9	11 - 10	2 - 9	3 - 8	4 - 7	5 - 6	

12 Team Schedule

1 - 12	4 - 2	2 - 11	3 - 10	4 - 9	5 - 8	6 - 7
1 - 2	3 - 12	4 - 11	5 - 10	6 - 9	7 - 8	1 - 3
5 - 12	6 - 11	7 - 10	8 - 9	1 - 4	5 - 3	6 - 2
7 - 12	8 - 11	9 - 10	1 - 5	6 - 4	7 - 3	8 - 2
9 - 12	10 - 11	1 - 5	7 - 4	8 - 3	9 - 2	10 - 1
11 - 12	1 - 7	8 - 6	9 - 5	10 - 4	11 - 3	12 - 2
1 - 8	9 - 7	10 - 6	11 - 5	12 - 4	2 - 3	1 - 9
10 - 8	11 - 7	12 - 6	2 - 5	3 - 4	1 - 10	11 - 9
12 - 8	2 - 7	3 - 6	4 - 5	1 - 11	12 - 10	2 - 9
3 - 8	4 - 7	5 - 6				

13 Team Schedule

1 - 12	8 - 9	2 - 11	3 - 10	4 - 9	5 - 8	6 - 7
1 - 13	3 - 12	4 - 11	5 - 10	6 - 9	7 - 8	6 - 2
4 - 13	5 - 12	6 - 11	7 - 10	1 - 3	5 - 2	6 - 13
7 - 12	8 - 11	9 - 10	1 - 4	6 - 3	7 - 2	8 - 13
9 - 12	10 - 11	1 - 5	7 - 4	8 - 3	9 - 2	10 - 13
11 - 12	1 - 6	8 - 5	9 - 4	10 - 3	11 - 2	12 - 13
1 - 7	9 - 6	10 - 5	11 - 4	12 - 3	13 - 2	1 - 8
10 - 7	11 - 6	12 - 5	13 - 4	2 - 3	1 - 9	11 - 8
12 - 7	13 - 6	2 - 5	3 - 4	1 - 10	12 - 9	13 - 8
2 - 7	3 - 6	4 - 5	1 - 11	13 - 10	13 - 12	2 - 11
3 - 10	4 - 9	5 - 8	6 - 7	3 - 9	3 - 8	4 - 7
5 - 6						

NOTES:

CHAPTER IX.

PREVENTION AND CARE OF INJURIES

1. Prevention and Care of Physical Education Class Injuries

2. Treatment of Injuries

3. Some Common Specific Injuries That Can Be Prevented

****

PREVENTION AND CARE OF PHYSICAL EDUCATION CLASS INJURIES

It should be a matter of common knowledge that any individual who is free from mental aberration and is structurally and organically sound should be capable of absorbing high dosage of vigorous physical activity without deleterious effects. It should be also obvious that no individual should be subjected to even moderately vigorous physical activity in the absence of a recent, medically administered, physical examination.

Before an instructor, administrator, or board of education permits physical education activities to be conducted under school auspices, the matter of moral and legal responsibility should be determined when medical examinations are not given periodically.

In reference to the normal, physically sound individual, legal and moral responsibilities are still present in the conduct of physical education activities. The instructor is responsible for teaching the activity in a safe and reasonable manner, so that no harm befalls his charges. The administration and board of education also assume responsibility in a similar manner through their delegation of authority to the instructor.

It is the purpose here to explore, to some degree, the responsibility of the instructor in relation to inherent injuries that may occur in classes involving physical activity of some vigorous nature. Any physical activity which puts added stress on the muscles, ligaments, or bones of the human body is, inherently, a potential source of injury. Such injuries may vary in degree from annoying muscle soreness to broken bones. In extreme cases crippling may occur or even death.

Injuries are very apt to happen with some frequency in those activities involving bodily contact, one with another, or contact of a single body with some object, such as the landing in a high jump activity, or running into a goal post in flag football.

From the standpoint of foreseeing and preventing possible injuries, the instructor should carefully check the playing area for hazardous conditions. Benches near the boundary lines of a running activity are matters of grave concern. Wet surfaces requiring friction for stopping, turning, or quick change of direction, such as in soccer or basketball, should evoke concern. Inadequate equipment, or unsafe apparatus is another hazard. To this list might be added uncovered steam pipes, broken bottles as the result of poor groundskeeping, unprotected corners, glass paneled doors in line of fast traffic, and mats too thin for the purpose intended. It is the duty of the instructor to notify his superior of such unsafe conditions. It would be advisable that such comments be made in writing with a copy retained by the instructor.

The instructor is directly responsible for so conducting the activity, in addition to safety considerations, that it is evident sound physiological measures are being followed. In this respect the instructor should be aware of the signs of physical duress that would caution him when to slow down or stop an activity. There is no excuse for using as punishment in a moment of anger the running of an unreasonable number of laps at the end of a hard session, when it is evident that the boy has already reached the point of exhaustion. The teacher should also know enough about the human anatomy to guide him properly in eliminating movements and body positions that might prove hazardous. All of this plays a part in the prevention of injuries.

Matters Concerning the Treatment of Injuries

Any teacher, especially the physical education teacher, is expected to have adequate knowledge of rendering first aid treatment to an injured individual. A thorough understanding, on the part of the instructor as to how far he should go in giving this aid and treatment is important. Just as important, is the knowedge of how far not to go. It would be wise for the instructor to check with an authority in the field of medicine, preferably a local physician on possible injuries that might be expected to occur in certain activities and under certain conditions. The physician might indicate, if he trusts your ability, a number of minor injuries you could safely deal with, without rushing each such case to his busy office. On the other hand, there would be injuries of certain types indicating the immediate attention of the physician.

SOME COMMON SPECIFIC INJURIES THAT CAN BE PREVENTED

There are some specific injuries that an instructor might expect to see during his teaching career, but which can, with some foresight and knowledge, be prevented. The following call attention to incidents of fairly frequent occurence.

Torn Muscle Tissue

Torn muscle tissue is technically called a muscle strain, which infers torn tissue due to overstretching of the muscle. A body part which is put through an extreme range of motion with force, is most apt to cause an excessive pull on a muscle tissue, resulting in a tearing of muscle fibers.

An example is in having beginners attempt headstands. When beginners invert the body and place their body weight on the head and neck, they are most apt to lose their balance and roll over on the back. When such a roll occurs the head is forcibly flexed with the chin pressing hard on the chest. This puts a forcible stretch on the muscles at the back of the neck and most likely the trapezius. The result of such movement often occurs in a painful injury in the area of the back of the neck, or, perhaps a bit lower. Obviously, the same type of injury may occur in the practice of forward rolls.

Injury to other muscles may occur in movements such as squat jumps, leg splits, etc., unless pre-stretching is first practiced.

Bones Broken at the Epiphysis

Bones grow and change shape at junctures called the "epiphysis." The epiphyses are cartilaginous tissue separating bone. As a child matures the cartilage forming the epiphysis ossifies, or changes from cartilage to bone. The epiphysis of long bones may not ossify until one reaches fifteen to twenty-four years of age. Since growth of bone takes place here, a break (or shearing due to stress) at such junction could be, conceivably, quite serious.

In building ground pyramids, the heavier members of the class are usually placed at the bottom. The instructor should be aware of the possible shearing of the proximal end of the tibia in students who are so placed and must bear a heavy load.

Head Injuries

Any rather severe blow to the head should provoke concern on the part of the instructor, even if a state of unconsciousness does not occur. It is not a rare occurrence for bleeding beneath the skull to follow blows on the head. It may take several hours for such bleeding to gain volume enough to cause subsequent unconsciousness denoting a severe injury. The possibility of bleeding beneath the skull following a blow prompts one to place the injured person under observation for twenty-four hours.

Instructor's Responsibility

Children usually are, and should be, the most prized possession of a set of parents. When an instructor takes thirty or forty youngsters under his care and supervision, he has indeed accepted a very grave responsibility. He must be absolutely sure he knows how to handle any contingency that may arise. If he is not sure, then he may have to live with the moral, if not legal, retribution connected with a negligent act in dealing with youngsters.

CHAPTER X.

CHECK LIST FOR A SAFE PHYSICAL

EDUCATION ENVIRONMENT

****

Check List for Safe Physical Education Environment

1. Are all activities supervised by staff members?

2. Has a plan of procedure been set up for the handling of accidents?

3. Are the rules for entering and leaving the physical education areas understood by all?

4. Are all persons, staff and students required to report injuries? and where?

5. Are staff meetings held regularly and attendance required?

6. Is an accurate record kept of injuries?

7. Has the school's liability been established and explained to all concerned?

8. Are telephone numbers available for parents, hospitals, doctors, fire department, and ambulance service?

9. Have objectives and goals been set up for the physical education program?

10. When students become sick or injured, have arrangements been made to get them home?

11. Are exposed corners and danger spots padded or otherwise protected?

12. Have precautions been taken with thermostats to prevent scalding in the showers?

13. Has anything been done to prevent slippery floors in the showers and dressing rooms?

14. Is bathing required and supervised?

15. Has a plan been worked out for clean towels and soap?

16. Do all inside areas have two exits apart from one another?

17. Is there ample fire protection?

18. Are flamables kept away from dressing rooms?

19. Are all exit doors operating properly and outward?

20. Are the exit signs conspicuous and lighted?

21. Are steps equipped with non-slip treads, in good repair, and have hand rails on the sides?

22. Are hot water heating boilers equipped with safety valves located far enough from area as to not constitute a hazard?

23. Do all exit doors have panic bars?

24. Are all areas adequately lighted?

25. Are all passage areas free from all obstructions all of the time?

26. Is there a distinctive fire alarm?

27. Have routines been established for emergencies?

28. Are the receptacles for drinking water adequate?

29. Are the drinking water receptacles kept clean?

30. Are fire extinguishers conveniently located?

31. Are the fire extinguishers checked at regular intervals and re-charged when needed?

32. Have all the staff and others in authority been given training in the operation of the safety devices?

33. Is there an understanding between custodians and staff as to duties and procedures?

34. Has a procedure been set up to properly issue and return equipment in good condition?

35. Has the equipment, particularly the protective devices, been checked to insure good condition?

36. Are there notices calling attention to possible hazards?

37. Are first aid areas identified and located centrally?

38. Is there good housekeeping ?

39. Is the first aid rendered by competent personnel?

40. Are hazardous conditions recognized and corrected as soon as possible?

41. Is the wearing of protective devices enforced where the activity so demands?

42. Is the supervision close enough to frown on clowning and horseplay so that it does not start?

43. Is equipment like ropes and gymnastic equipment inspected regularly?

44. Are medical examinations required of all and at regular intervals?

45. Does the instruction call attention to possible hazards and take steps to lessen them?

46. Are grounds patrolled regularly to pick up glass, rocks, and other rough materials?

47. Are switch boxes kept locked and available only to authorized personnel?

48. When transportation is necessary is it adequate and approved?

49. Has the cooperation of the state, municipalities, and organizations interested in safety been consulted and asked to cooperate?

50. Is a good insurance program available to all persons participating in the physical program?

CHAPTER XI.

GENERAL PHYSICAL EDUCATION HEALTH

AND SPORT ACTIVITY TESTS

****

GENERAL PHYSICAL EDUCATION TEST

(This test or parts of it may be given at the end of the year after all the clothing has been checked in. It will measure somewhat the student's general knowledge of sports and health topics that may have been mentioned during the COMMENTARY ON RELATED ACTIVITIES. It would not seem to be a fair basis for **grading** in itself, but should rather be considered a measurement of the material covered by the instructor during the year. This is just a sample. Many more items may easily be included.)

1. How many bones are in the ear?

2. Flat feet are always painful?

3. Good fitting shoes help offset the pain of flat feet?

4. Hammer .. anvil .. stirrup refer to what part of the body?

5. People who are nearsighted have "short eyes."

6. Sun glasses are necessary for all people who work outside.

7. Badminton rackets are heavier than tennis rackets.

8. Badminton nets are lower in the middle than on the sides.

9. The common way to stop bleeding is by applying pressure.

10. Toe nails should be cut straight across.

11. Only boys and men get athletes foot, women are immune.

12. Tourniquets must be released every few minutes otherwise they will do more harm than good.

13. Accident victims should be immediately moved, then examined.

14. The most common source of carbon monoxide gas poisoning is the auto exhaust.

15. Colds are contagious through coughing and sneezing.

16. Disposable tissues properly used are more sanitary than handkerchiefs.

17. Candy is a good source of energy.

18. Candy is the only source of energy.

19. The proper time to eat candy is probably after meals.

20. With perfect brakes on an auto and a person with good reflexes, a car going twenty miles an hour can not stop in much less than forty-five feet.

21. There are no longer automobiles in existence which are over fifty years old which are in running condition.

22. The Indianapolis Speedway is paved with bricks under the surfacing.

23. Racing cars on the Indianapolis Speedway travel clockwise.

24. Most wounds with dirt involved should be washed with soap and water.

25. Rest is essential in the treatment of a cold.

26. Chilling the body tends to cause the "common cold."

27. Body cleanliness is an aid to keeping healthy.

28. The starting point in golf is the "green."

29. Golf should not be played in groups larger than four.

30. Lost golf balls are never looked for because it holds up play.

31. Picking up marbles with ones toes is considered a good exercise for flat feet.

32. When driving on ice speed is not dangerous as long as the brake is not used.

33. With good average lights sixty-five miles per hour is safe at night.

34. People under twenty-five tend to have more auto accidents than those over twenty-five.

35. The first step in first aid is to make the victim comfortable.

36. Good posture makes for good health.

37. Running in the snow barefooted is a good way to keep from getting cold feet.

38. Cutting the hair helps to make it grow.

39. The best cure for a charleyhorse is vigorous exercise.

40. Athlete's foot is a fungus disease.

41. In what part of the body are the sinus cavities?

42. The army does not believe in setting up exercises.

43. Good training for athletes consists merely in living as we should anyway.

44. All words ending in "itis" refer to inflamation.

45. The hot bath should be followed by a cold one.

46. After the bath the arms should be dried first.

47. Floor burns from basketball and like sports are best treated by splashing on alcohol.

48. The weight of a person is usually a good index to his general health.

49. The warning signal for golf is BALL.

50. In a 10 team tourney there are 6 byes.

51. The basketball hoop is 12 feet high.

52. The free throw line is 12 feet from the bankboard.

53. A regulation basketball floor if fifty feet wide.

54. The basketball rules require that numbers be on both the back and front of the playing jersey.

55. The highest jumper always gets the tip in basketball.

56. On most floors there is four feet behind the plane of the bankboard in basketball.

57. A baseball diamond is square.

58. It is seventy-five feet from first base to second base in baseball.

59. Home plate is outside the area referred to as the diamond.

60. The average pulse rate of an adult is about 118.

61. An adult's blood pressure should be about 110 plus 1/2 the age.

62. Arteries carry blood away from the heart.

63. Veins carry blood back to the heart.

64. The blood of anyone can be used by anyone else for transfusion.

65. In parking an auto it is best to enter the space going forward.

66. There are eight games in an eight team tourney with a consolation game.

67. Being runnerup in a tourney is the same as coming in last.

68. The mile has been run in less than four minutes.

69. How many 440 yard runs must one travel to cover a distance of two miles?

70. If a person were drowning, close to shore, it usually would be better to throw a rope to him rather than to swim out to make the rescue.

71. What is called the perfect food?

72. In weight lifting exercises use about one half your weight in determining how much weight should be used by a beginner.

73. What is the common name for poliomyelitis?

74. In tennis the score is tied when it is DEUCE.

75. In the ordinary nosebleed, lie down on the back, head a little low.

76. An allergy is a sensitivity to a substance harmless to most people.

77. Self-preservation is the first instinct of man.

78. One could win a football game 1 to 0.

79. One could win a basketball game 1 to 0.

80. Sash cord makes a good jump rope.

81. Sash cord makes good rope for twirling.

82. There is approximately 15 pounds of air in a basketball.

83. Relays are a method of learning skills under competitive conditions.

84. Frostbite is more likely to occur in damp and windy weather.

85. The best time ever run for the one-half mile is under two minutes.

86. If you are myopic, you are farsighted.

87. The basketball circle at the center has the same diameter as those at the free throw areas.

88. Crampon refers to what sport?_____

89. Divot refers to what sport?_____

90. Torpedo head refers to what sport?_____

91. Parlay refers to what sport?

92. Vorlage refers to what sport?

93. Pike refers to what sport?

94. Riposte refers to what sport?

95. Scrum refers to what sport?

96. Quiver refers to what sport?

97. Cushions refers to what sport?

98. Wickets (Eng.) refers to what sport?

99. Jib refers to what sport?

100. What activites would you recommend be added to the physical education program?

NOTE: It is suggested that a series of questions to added to the above that would apply to the class material that has been covered.

General Physical Education Test .. (Answers)

1. Three
2. False
3. True
4. Ear
5. True
6. False
7. False
8. True
9. True
10. True
11. False
12. True
13. False
14. True
15. True
16. True
17. True
18. False
19. True
20. True
21. False
22. True
23. False
24. True
25. True
26. False ?
27. True
28. False
29. True
30. False
31. True
32. False
33. False
34. True
35. True
36. True
37. False
38. False
39. False
40. True

41. Head
42. False
43. True
44. True
45. True
46. False
47. False
48. True
49. False
50. True
51. False
52. False
53. True
54. True
55. False
56. True
57. True
58. False
59. False
60. False
61. True
62. True
63. False
64. False
65. False
66. True
67. False
68. True
69. Eight
70. True
71. Milk
72. False
73. Polio
74. True
75. True
76. True
77. True
78. False
79. True
80. True

81. True
82. False
83. True
84. True
85. True
86. False
87. True
88. Mountain climbing
89. Golf
90. Fly fishing
91. Horse racing
92. Skiing
93. Diving - fish
94. Fencing
95. Rugby
96. Archery
97. Billiards
98. Cricket
99. Sailing
100. To be appraised by the instructor

knit in a day for baby

LEISURE ARTS STAFF
President and Chief Executive Officer
Rick Barton

Vice President of Editorial
Susan White Sullivan

Vice President of Sales
Mike Behar

National Sales Director
Martha Adams

Vice President of Finance and Administration
Laticia Dittrich

Controller
Francis Caple

Vice President of Operations
Jim Dittrich

Retail Customer Service Manager
Stan Raynor

Vice President of Purchasing
Fred F. Pruss

Information Technology Director
Hermine Linz

Director of eCommerce-Prepress Services
Mark Hawkins

PRODUCED FOR LEISURE ARTS, INC. BY
Candice Jensen Productions
Editor: Heather Vantress
Design and layout: Rita Sowins / Sowins Design
Technical editing: Sandi Rosner
Photography by: Silvana Di Franco

Printed In China

ISBN: 978-1-4647-0264-8

Library of Congress Control Number: 2012934866

knit in a day
for baby

✳ **20** ✳
Quick & Easy
Projects

Candi Jensen

Photography by: Silvana Di Franco

LEISURE ARTS
the art of everyday living
www.leisurearts.com

contents

Introduction

"Patterns labeled 'quick and easy baby knits' have always seemed a little illusive to me, because I can end up spending many more hours than I expected. In this book, I'm bringing you basic patterns that you really can work up in a day, plus 'upgrades' for those occasions when you have a little more time.

This idea actually came about because of a baby shower. I wanted to knit up something special, but only thought about it at the last minute. You can literally start some of the projects in this book the night before and show up with a lovely handmade gift that will impress. You don't have to admit that it was a last minute project! The smaller projects, like washcloths or booties, are a great handmade addition to something ready-made.

I encourage you to change up the colors within the patterns. With the dot pullover, for instance, make each dot a different color and put on as many as you like. Or put dots on the cardigan and stripes on the pullover. Have fun with the projects and make them your own.

Most of all I want you to enjoy making these fun designs for little ones. Every baby is special and deserving of special hand knits."

—Candi Jensen

pullovers

"Pullover sweaters are a basic for Baby's wardrobe. Perfect for playtime or dress up, they will be cherished and worn day after day.

The sweaters in this section are knit at a nice chunky gauge so they work up quickly. The garter stitch border gives wonderful texture, and is easier and faster than ribbing. A placket at the neck makes for a much bigger opening, so you won't have to struggle to get it over a baby's head. We all know how much babies hate that!

The basic pullover has raglan sleeves, which provide baby with more room to move those busy little arms. I chose to work it in two colors, but you could just as easily stitch it up in one color.

Our second pullover has a wider garter stitch border on both the sleeves and the lower edge to give it a bit more texture.

Finally, the pink and white pullover offers a bit more challenge, but is still quite easy. The duplicate stitch dots take a little more time but add a bunch more character and fun. The idea is to have fun. Feel free to put your own stamp on the sweater."

green & white pullover

Easy ✹ ✹ ✵ ✵

Sizes:
6 (12, 18, 24) months
Instructions are for size 6 months. Changes for sizes 12, 18 and 24 months are in parentheses.

Finished Measurements:
Chest: 20 (22, 24, 26)"
Length: 11 (12, 13, 14)"

Materials:
* Worsted weight (**4** medium) yarn, 3½ oz / 100g (approx 175 yds / 156m)
* Color A: 1 skein light green; approx. 40 (50, 60, 75) yds
* Color B: 2 (3, 3, 4) skeins ivory; approx 320 (400, 475, 550) yds
* 2 small stitch holders, 4 medium stitch holders
* 2 buttons ⅝" / 16mm

Needles:
* Size 11 / 8mm or size to obtain gauge for body
* Size 10½ / 6.5mm for edging
* Large eye yarn needle

Gauge:
12 sts & 16 rows = 4" / 10 cm in St st using double strand of yarn and larger needles

Notes:
Work with 2 strands of yarn held together throughout.
While working striped edgings, do not cut the yarn when changing colors. Carry the yarn not in use loosely up the side of the piece.

Back

With smaller needles and 2 strands of color A held together, cast on 32 (35, 38, 41) sts. Knit 2 rows. Change to 2 strands of color B held together and knit 2 rows. Change to color A and knit 2 rows. Cut color A. Change to larger needles.
With color B, starting with a knit row, work in St st until piece measures 7 (7½, 8, 8½)", ending with a WS row.

SHAPE ARMHOLES
Bind off 2 sts at the beginning of the next 2 rows.
Next row (RS): K1, ssk, knit to last 3 sts, k2tog, k1.
Next row (WS): Purl.
Repeat last 2 rows 6 (7, 8, 9) more times—14 (15, 16, 17) sts remain. Place on a stitch holder.

Front

Work same as Back to armholes.

SHAPE ARMHOLES
Bind off 2 sts at the beginning of the next 2 rows.
Next row (RS): K1, ssk, knit to last 3 sts, k2tog, k1.
Next row (WS): Purl.
Repeat last 2 rows 4 (5, 6, 7) more times—18 (19, 20, 21) sts remain.

SHAPE NECK
Row 1 (RS): K1, ssk, k2, place remaining 13 (14, 15, 16) sts on stitch holder.
Row 2 (WS): Purl
Row 3: K1, k2tog, k1.
Row 4: Purl. Place remaining 3 stitches on stitch holder.
Join yarn to neck stitches on holder.
Row 1 (RS): K10 (11, 12, 13), k2tog, k1.
Row 2(WS): P4, place remaining 8 (9, 10, 11) sts on holder.
Row 3: K1, ssk, k1.
Row 4: Purl. Place remaining 3 sts on holder.

Sleeves (make 2)

With smaller needles and 2 strands of color A held together, cast on 17 (20, 23, 26) sts. Knit 2 rows. Change to 2 strands of color B held together and knit 2 rows. Change to color A and knit 2 rows. Cut color A. Change to larger needles.

With color B, starting with a knit row, work 6 rows in St st.

Next row (RS): K1, kfb, knit to last st, kfb, k1.

Work 5 rows in St st.

Next row (RS): K1, kfb, knit to last st, kfb, k1—21 (24, 27, 30) sts.

Continue without shaping until piece measures 6 (6½, 7, 7½)", ending with a WS row.

SHAPE SLEEVE CAP

Bind off 2 sts at the beginning of the next 2 rows.

Next row (RS): K1, ssk, knit to last 3 sts, k2tog, k1.

Next row (WS): Purl.

Repeat last 2 rows 6 (7, 8, 9) more times. Place remaining 3 (4, 5, 6) sts on holder.

Finishing

Sew sleeves to back armholes. Sew right sleeve to front at armhole. Sew left sleeve to front at armhole, leaving top 3" of seam open for buttonhole band. Sew side seams. Sew sleeve seams.

BUTTONHOLE BAND

With RS facing, using smaller needles and 2 strands of color A held together, pick up and knit 10 sts along angled edge of front left armhole. Knit 1 row.

Next row – buttonhole row (RS): K2, k2tog, yo, k3, k2tog, yo, k1.

Knit 1 row. Bind off, but do not fasten off final loop or cut yarn.

NECKBAND

With RS facing, using smaller needles and 2 strands of color A held together, place final loop from buttonhole band on needle, pick up and knit 1 st at side of buttonhole band, knit 3 from holder at left front, knit 8 (9, 10, 11) from holder at center front, knit 3 from holder at right front, knit 3 (4, 5, 6) from holder at right sleeve, knit 14 (15, 16, 17) from holder at back neck, knit 3 (4, 5, 6) from holder at left sleeve—36 (40, 44, 48) sts. Knit 1 WS row. Bind off.

Sew buttons to left sleeve cap to correspond to buttonholes

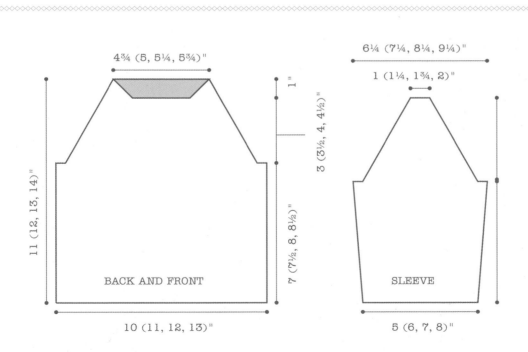

4¾ (5, 5¼, 5¾)"

6¼ (7¼, 8¼, 9¼)"

1 (1¼, 1¾, 2)"

1"

3 (3½, 4, 4½)"

11 (12, 13, 14)"

7 (7½, 8, 8½)"

BACK AND FRONT

SLEEVE

10 (11, 12, 13)"

5 (6, 7, 8)"

basic pullover— gray trim

Sizes:

6 (12, 18, 24) months

Instructions are for size 6 months. Changes for sizes 12, 18 and 24 months are in parentheses.

Finished Measurements:

Chest: 20 (22, 24, 26)"

Length: 11 (12, 13, 14)"

Materials:

* Worsted weight (❨4❩ medium) yarn, 3½ oz / 100g (approx 175 yds / 156m)
* Color A: 1 skein gray; approx. 60 (70, 80, 90) yds
* Color B: 2 (3, 3, 4) skeins ivory; approx. 320 (400, 475, 550) yds
* 2 small stitch holders, 4 medium stitch holders
* 2 buttons ⅝" / 16mm

Needles:

* Size 11 / 8mm or size to obtain gauge for body
* Size 10½ / 6.5mm for edging
* Large eye yarn needle

Gauge:

12 sts & 16 rows = 4" / 10 cm in St st using double strand of yarn and larger needles

Notes:

Work with 2 strands of yarn held together throughout.

While working striped edgings, do not cut the yarn when changing colors. Carry the yarn not in use loosely up the side of the piece.

Back

With smaller needles and 2 strands of color A held together, cast on 32 (35, 38, 41) sts. Knit 2 rows. * Change to 2 strands of color B held together and knit 2 rows. Change to color A and knit 2 rows. Repeat from * 2 more times. Cut color A. Change to larger needles.

With color B, starting with a knit row, work in St st until piece measures 7 (7½, 8, 8½)", ending with a WS row.

SHAPE ARMHOLES

Bind off 2 sts at the beginning of the next 2 rows.

Next row (RS): K1, ssk, knit to last 3 sts, k2tog, k1.

Next row (WS): Purl.

Repeat last 2 rows 6 (7, 8, 9) more times—14 (15, 16, 17) sts remain. Place on a stitch holder.

Front

Work same as Back to armholes.

SHAPE ARMHOLES

Bind off 2 sts at the beginning of the next 2 rows.

Next row (RS): K1, ssk, knit to last 3 sts, k2tog, k1.

Next row (WS): Purl.

Repeat last 2 rows 4 (5, 6, 7) more times—18 (19, 20, 21) sts remain.

SHAPE NECK

Row 1 (RS): K1, ssk, k2, place remaining 13 (14, 15, 16) sts on stitch holder.

Row 2 (WS): Purl

Row 3: K1, k2tog, k1.

Row 4: Purl. Place remaining 3 stitches on stitch holder.

Join yarn to neck stitches on holder.

Row 1 (RS): K10 (11, 12, 13), k2tog, k1.

Row 2(WS): P4, place remaining 8 (9, 10, 11) sts on holder.

Row 3: K1, ssk, k1.

Row 4: Purl. Place remaining 3 sts on holder.

Sleeves (make 2)

With smaller needles and 2 strands of color A held together, cast on 17 (20, 23, 26) sts. Knit 2 rows. * Change to 2 strands of color B held together and knit 2 rows. Change to color A and knit 2 rows. Repeat from * 2 more times. Cut color A. Change to larger needles.

With color B, starting with a knit row, work 6 rows in St st.

Next row (RS): K1, kfb, knit to last st, kfb, k1.

Work 5 rows in St st.

Next row (RS): K1, kfb, knit to last st, kfb, k1—21 (24, 27, 30) sts.

Continue without shaping until piece measures 6 (6½, 7, 7½)", ending with a WS row.

SHAPE SLEEVE CAP

Bind off 2 sts at the beginning of the next 2 rows.

Next row (RS): K1, ssk, knit to last 3 sts, k2tog, k1.

Next row (WS): Purl.

Repeat last 2 rows 6 (7, 8, 9) more times. Place remaining 3 (4, 5, 6) sts on holder.

Finishing

Sew sleeves to back armholes. Sew right sleeve to front at armhole. Sew left sleeve to front at armhole, leaving top 3" of seam open for buttonhole band. Sew side seams. Sew sleeve seams.

BUTTONHOLE BAND

With RS facing, using smaller needles and 2 strands of color A held together, pick up and knit 10 sts along angled edge of front left armhole. Knit 1 row.

Next row – buttonhole row (RS): K2, k2tog, yo, k3, k2tog, yo, k1.

Knit 1 row. Bind off, but do not fasten off final loop or cut yarn.

NECKBAND

With RS facing, using smaller needles and 2 strands of color A held together, place final loop from buttonhole band on needle, pick up and knit 1 st at side of buttonhole band, knit 3 from holder at left front, knit 8 (9, 10, 11) from holder at center front, knit 3 from holder at right front, knit 3 (4, 5, 6) from holder at right sleeve, knit 14 (15, 16, 17) from holder at back neck, knit 3 (4, 5, 6) from holder at left sleeve—36 (40, 44, 48) sts. Knit 1 WS row. Bind off.

Sew buttons to left sleeve cap to correspond to buttonholes.

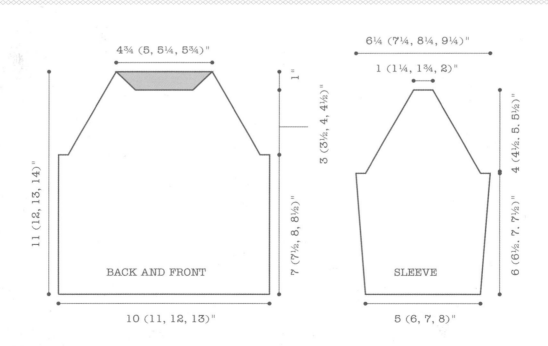

BACK AND FRONT

4¾ (5, 5¼, 5¾)"

11 (12, 13, 14)"

10 (11, 12, 13)"

1"

3 (3½, 4, 4½)"

7 (7½, 8, 8½)"

SLEEVE

6¼ (7¼, 8¼, 9¼)"

1 (1¼, 1¾, 2)"

4 (4½, 5, 5½)"

6 (6½, 7, 7½)"

5 (6, 7, 8)"

basic pullover— pink dots

Sizes:

6 (12, 18, 24) months
Instructions are for size 6 months. Changes for sizes 12, 18 and 24 months are in parentheses.

Finished Measurements:

Chest: 20 (22, 24, 26)"
Length: 11 (12, 13, 14)"

Materials:

* Worsted weight (**4** medium) yarn, 3½ oz / 100g (approx 175 yds / 156m)
* Color A: 1 skein pink; approx. 60 (70, 80, 90) yds
* Color B: 2 (3, 3, 4) skeins ivory; approx. 320 (400, 475, 550) yds
* 2 small stitch holders, 4 medium stitch holders
* 2 buttons ⅝" / 16mm

Needles:

* Size 11 / 8mm or size to obtain gauge for body
* Size 10½ / 6.5mm for edging
* Large eye yarn needle

Gauge:

12 sts & 16 rows = 4" / 10 cm in St st using double strand of yarn and larger needles

Notes:

Work with 2 strands of yarn held together throughout.
While working striped edgings, do not cut the yarn when changing colors. Carry the yarn not in use loosely up the side of the piece.

Back

With smaller needles and 2 strands of color A held together, cast on 32 (35, 38, 41) sts. Knit 2 rows. Change to 2 strands of color B held together and knit 2 rows. Change to color A and knit 2 rows. Cut color A.
Change to larger needles.
With color B, starting with a knit row, work in St st until piece measures 7 (7½, 8, 8½)", ending with a WS row.

SHAPE ARMHOLES

Bind off 2 sts at the beginning of the next 2 rows.
Next row (RS): K1, ssk, knit to last 3 sts, k2tog, k1.
Next row (WS): Purl.
Repeat last 2 rows 6 (7, 8, 9) more times—14 (15, 16, 17) sts remain. Place on a stitch holder.

Front

Work same as Back to armholes.

SHAPE ARMHOLES

Bind off 2 sts at the beginning of the next 2 rows.

Next row (RS): K1, ssk, knit to last 3 sts, k2tog, k1.
Next row (WS): Purl.
Repeat last 2 rows 4 (5, 6, 7) more times—18 (19, 20, 21) sts remain.

SHAPE NECK

Row 1 (RS): K1, ssk, k2, place remaining 13 (14, 15, 16) sts on stitch holder.
Row 2 (WS): Purl
Row 3: K1, k2tog, k1.
Row 4: Purl. Place remaining 3 stitches on stitch holder.
Join yarn to neck stitches on holder.
Row 1 (RS): K10 (11, 12, 13), k2tog, k1.
Row 2(WS): P4, place remaining 8 (9, 10, 11) sts on holder.
Row 3: K1, ssk, k1.
Row 4: Purl. Place remaining 3 sts on holder.

Sleeves (make 2)

With smaller needles and 2 strands of color A held together, cast on 17 (20, 23, 26) sts. Knit 2 rows. Change to 2 strands of color B held together and knit 2 rows. Change to color A and knit 2 rows. Cut color A.

Change to larger needles.

With color B, starting with a knit row, work 6 rows in St st.

Next row (RS): K1, kfb, knit to last st, kfb, k1.

Work 5 rows in St st.

Next row (RS): K1, kfb, knit to last st, kfb, k1—21 (24, 27, 30) sts.

Continue without shaping until piece measures 6 (6½, 7, 7½)", ending with a WS row.

SHAPE SLEEVE CAP

Bind off 2 sts at the beginning of the next 2 rows.

Next row (RS): K1, ssk, knit to last 3 sts, k2tog, k1.

Next row (WS): Purl.

Repeat last 2 rows 6 (7, 8, 9) more times. Place remaining 3 (4, 5, 6) sts on holder.

Finishing

EMBROIDERY

Use 2 strands of color A held together to work dot chart using duplicate stitch. Place dots at random on front, back and sleeves.

Sew sleeves to back armholes. Sew right sleeve to front at armhole. Sew left sleeve to front at armhole, leaving top 3" of seam open for buttonhole band. Sew side seams. Sew sleeve seams.

BUTTONHOLE BAND

With RS facing, using smaller needles and 2 strands of color B held together, pick up and knit 10 sts along angled edge of front left armhole. Knit 1 row.

Next row – buttonhole row (RS): K2, k2tog, yo, k3, k2tog, yo, k1.

Knit 1 row. Bind off, but do not fasten off final loop or cut yarn.

NECKBAND

With RS facing, using smaller needles and 2 strands of color B held together, place final loop from buttonhole band on needle, pick up and knit 1 st at side of buttonhole band, knit 3 from holder at left front, knit 8 (9, 10, 11) from holder at center front, knit 3 from holder at right front, knit 3 (4, 5, 6) from holder at right sleeve, knit 14 (15, 16, 17) from holder at back neck, knit 3 (4, 5, 6) from holder at left sleeve—36 (40, 44, 48) sts. Knit 1 WS row. Bind off.

Sew buttons to left sleeve cap to correspond to buttonholes.

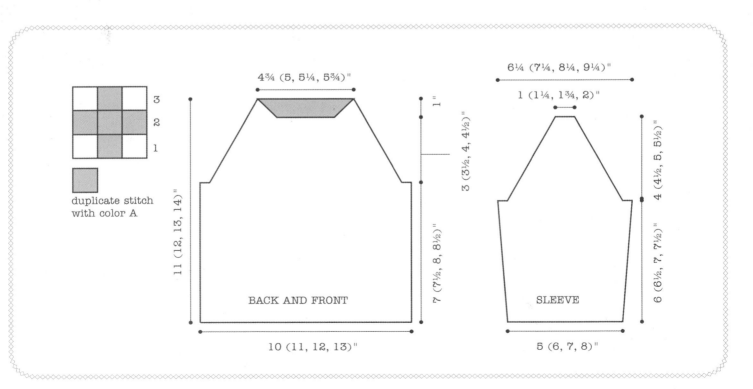

duplicate stitch with color A

4¾ (5, 5¼, 5¾)"

1"

3 (3½, 4, 4½)"

11 (12, 13, 14)"

7 (7½, 8, 8½)"

BACK AND FRONT

10 (11, 12, 13)"

6¼ (7¼, 8¼, 9¼)"

1 (1¼, 1¾, 2)"

4 (4½, 5, 5½)"

6 (6½, 7, 7½)"

SLEEVE

5 (6, 7, 8)"

✺ cardigans ✺

"Cardigans are great for layering and can be used year-round. They are perfect over a summer dress, to pair with overalls, or to bundle up if the weather turns cold. I am especially fond of cardigans for their versatility, though they take just a bit more time to make than a pullover.

Even though the basic cardigan is worked in two colors, you should be able to make all the pieces in a day. It is stitched in a chunky gauge and in one piece to the armholes, so there are no side seams to sew up.

If you have just a little more time, you might want to think about adding stripes, as in the second cardigan. It takes a bit more effort to carry the yarn, but it makes a very distinctive sweater.

With that extra time, you may wish to add a pattern stitch for texture as in the third sweater. Although it uses the same basic pattern, this one has a rounded neck, allowing you to add even more variety to the basic cardigan."

green & white cardigan

Easy ✸ ✸ ✸ ✸

Sizes:

6 (12, 18, 24) months
Instructions are for size 6 months. Changes for sizes 12, 18 and 24 months are in parentheses.

Finished Measurements:

Chest: 19¾ (22¼, 25, 27¾)"
Length: 10½ (12, 13, 14)"

Materials:

* Worsted weight (**4** medium) yarn, 3½ oz /100g (approx 175 yds / 156m)
* Color A: 1 skein light green; approx. 40 (50, 60, 75) yds
* Color B: 2 (2, 3, 3) skeins ivory; approx. 225 (280, 340, 400) yds
* 2 small and 3 medium stitch holders
* 3 (4, 5, 6) wooden buttons ¾" / 20mm

Needles:

* Size 11 / 8mm or size to obtain gauge
* Large eye yarn needle

Gauge:

12 sts & 16 rows = 4" / 10 cm in St st using double strand of yarn

K1 P1 Rib:

Worked over an odd number of stitches:
Row 1 (RS): P1, * k1, p1; repeat from * to end.
Row 2 (WS): K1, * p1, k1; repeat from * to end.

Notes:

Work with 2 strands of yarn held together throughout.

Body

With 2 strands of color A held together, cast on 59 (67, 75, 83) sts. Work 4 rows in K1 P1 Rib.
Next row (RS): * P1, k1; repeat from * once and place these 4 sts on a stitch holder, change to 2 strands of color B held together and k 51 (59, 67, 75), place remaining 4 sts on a stitch holder.
Work even on remaining 51 (59, 67, 75) sts until piece measures 6½ (7½, 8, 8½)", ending with a WS row.

DIVIDE FOR FRONTS AND BACK

Next row (RS): K10 (12, 14, 16) sts and place on a stitch holder for Right Front, bind off 4 sts for right armhole, k23 (27, 31, 35) sts and place on a stitch holder for Back, bind off 4 sts for left armhole, knit to end—10 (12, 14, 16) stitches remain for Left Front.

Left Front

SHAPE NECK

Next row (WS): Purl.
Next row (RS): Knit to last 2 sts, k2tog—9 (11, 13, 15) sts remain.

Repeat last 2 rows 3 (4, 5, 7) more times—6 (7, 8, 8) sts remain.
Work even in St st until piece measures 10½ (12, 13, 14)".
Bind off.

Back

With WS facing, slip Back sts from holder to needle and join yarn—23 (27, 31, 35) sts.
Beginning with a WS row, work in St st until piece measures 10½ (12, 13, 14)".
Bind off.

Right Front

With WS facing, slip Right Front sts from holder to needle and join yarn.

SHAPE NECK

Next row (WS): Purl.
Next row (RS): Ssk, knit to end—9 (11, 13, 15) sts remain.
Repeat last 2 rows 3 (4, 5, 7) more times—6 (7, 8, 8) sts remain.
Work even in St st until piece measures 10½ (12, 13, 14)".
Bind off.

Sleeves (make 2)

With 2 strands of color A held together, cast on 18 (20, 22, 24) sts. Work 4 rows in K1 P1 Rib.

Change to 2 strands of color B held together.

Beginning with a WS row, work 3 rows in St st.

Next row(RS): K1, kfb, knit to last 2 sts, kfb, k1—20 (22, 24, 26) sts.

Work 5 rows in St st.

Repeat last 6 rows 3 (3, 4, 5) more times—26 (28, 32, 36) sts.

Work even in St st until piece measures 7 (8½, 10, 11)".

Bind off loosely.

Pocket

With 2 strands of color B held together, cast on 9 (9, 11, 13) sts. Work in St st until piece measures 2 (2½, 3, 3½)", ending with a WS row. Change to 2 strands of color A held together and knit 1 row. Bind off.

Finishing

Sew shoulder seams. Sew sleeve seams, leaving ¾" at top of sleeve open. Sew sleeves into armholes, sewing open section of sleeve seam to bound-off stitches at underarm.

Pin pocket to right front, placing it 2 sts away from front edge and 4 rows above lower ribbing. Sew in place.

BUTTONBAND

Slip ribbing stitches from holder at Left Front to needle. Work in K1 P1 Rib until band is long enough to reach center back neck. Return sts to holder.

Mark position for 3 (4, 5, 6) buttonholes along Right Front edge, with top buttonhole at beginning of neck shaping, bottom buttonhole at stitch holder, and remaining buttonholes evenly spaced between.

Slip ribbing stitches from holder at Right Front to needle. Work 1 WS row in K1 P1 Rib.

Next row – buttonhole row (RS): P1, ssk, yo, k1.

Continue in K1 P1 Rib, repeating buttonhole row at each marked position, until band is long enough to reach center back neck. Return sts to holder.

Sew bands to front edges, easing band to fit around neck shaping. Continue sewing bands to back neck edge. Adjust length of bands by adding or removing rows if necessary to make them fit smoothly. Bind off both bands and sew ends together.

Sew buttons to Left Front to correspond with buttonholes.

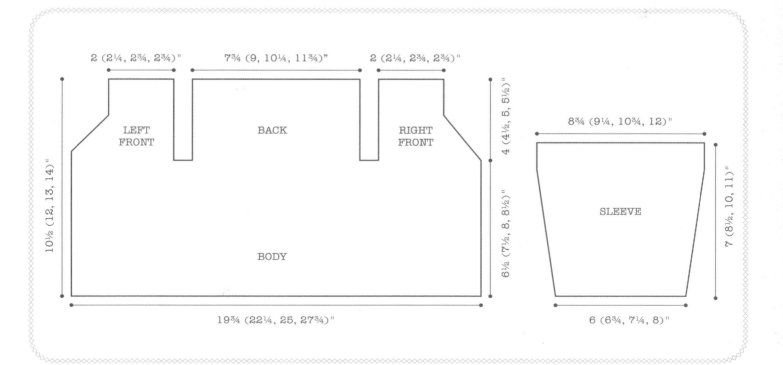

two color cardigan

Intermediate ✳ ✳ ✳ ✧

Sizes:
6 (12, 18, 24) months
Instructions are for size 6 months. Changes for sizes 12, 18 and 24 months are in parentheses.

Finished Measurements:
Chest: 19¾ (22¼, 25, 27¾)"
Length: 10½ (12, 13, 14)"

Materials:
* Worsted weight (**4** medium) yarn, 3½ oz /100g (approx 175 yds / 156m)
* Color A: 1 (2, 2, 2) skeins ivory; approx. 150 (200, 240, 285) yds
* Color B: 1 (1, 1, 2) skeins light blue; approx. 115 (130, 160, 190) yds
* 2 small and 3 medium stitch holders
* 3 (4, 5, 6) wooden buttons ¾" / 20mm

Needles:
* Size 11 / 8mm or size to obtain gauge
* Large eye yarn needle

Gauge:
12 sts & 16 rows = 4" / 10 cm in St st using double strand of yarn

K1 P1 Rib:
Worked over an odd number of stitches:
Row 1 (RS): P1, * k1, p1; repeat from * to end.
Row 2 (WS): K1, * p1, k1; repeat from * to end.

Notes:
Work with 2 strands of yarn held together throughout.

Body

With 2 strands of color A held together, cast on 59 (67, 75, 83) sts. Work 4 rows in K1 P1 Rib.
Next row (RS): * P1, k1; repeat from * once and place these 4 sts on a stitch holder, k 51 (59, 67, 75), place remaining 4 sts on a stitch holder.
Work 3 more rows in St st over remaining 51 (59, 67, 75) sts.
Change to 2 strands of color B held together and work 4 rows St st.
Continue alternating 4 rows of color A with 4 rows of color B for remainder of piece.
Work even until piece measures 6½ (7½, 8, 8½)", ending with a WS row.

DIVIDE FOR FRONTS AND BACK

Next row (RS): K10 (12, 14, 16) sts and place on a stitch holder for Right Front, bind off 4 sts for right armhole, k23 (27, 31, 35) sts and place on a stitch holder for Back, bind off 4 sts for left armhole, knit to end—10 (12, 14, 16) stitches remain for Left Front.

Left Front

SHAPE NECK

Next row (WS): Purl.
Next row (RS): Knit to last 2 sts, k2tog—9 (11, 13, 15) sts remain.
Repeat last 2 rows 3 (4, 5, 7) more times—6 (7, 8, 8) sts remain.
Work even in St st until piece measures 10½ (12, 13, 14)".
Bind off.

Back

With WS facing, slip Back sts from holder to needle and join yarn—23 (27, 31, 35) sts.
Beginning with a WS row, work in St st until piece measures 10½ (12, 13, 14)".
Bind off.

Right Front

With WS facing, slip Right Front sts from holder to needle and join yarn.

SHAPE NECK

Next row (WS): Purl.

Next row (RS): Ssk, knit to end—9 (11, 13, 15) sts remain.

Repeat last 2 rows 3 (4, 5, 7) more times—6 (7, 8, 8) sts remain.

Work even in St st until piece measures 10½ (12, 13, 14)".

Bind off.

Sleeves (make 2)

With 2 strands of color A held together, cast on 18 (20, 22, 24) sts. Work 4 rows in K1 P1 Rib.

Beginning with a WS row, work 3 rows in St st.

Next row- increase row (RS): K1, kfb, knit to last 2 sts, kfb, k1—20 (22, 24, 26) sts.

Change to 2 strands of color B held together. Work 4 rows in St st.

Continue alternating 4 rows of color A with 4 rows of color B for remainder of piece.

At the same time, repeat the increase row every 6th row 3 (3, 4, 5) more times—26 (28, 32, 36) sts.

Work even in St st until piece measures 7 (8½, 10, 11)".

Bind off loosely.

Finishing

Sew shoulder seams. Sew sleeve seams, leaving ¾" at top of sleeve open. Sew sleeves into armholes, sewing open section of sleeve seam to bound-off stitches at underarm.

BUTTONBAND

Slip ribbing stitches from holder at Left Front to needle. Work in K1 P1 Rib until band is long enough to reach center back neck. Return sts to holder.

Mark position for 3 (4, 5, 6) buttonholes along Right Front edge, with top buttonhole at beginning of neck shaping, bottom buttonhole at stitch holder, and remaining buttonholes evenly spaced between.

Slip ribbing stitches from holder at Right Front to needle. Work 1 WS row in K1 P1 Rib.

Next row – buttonhole row (RS): P1, ssk, yo, k1.

Continue in K1 P1 Rib, repeating buttonhole row at each marked position, until band is long enough to reach center back neck. Return sts to holder.

Sew bands to front edges, easing band to fit around neck shaping. Continue sewing bands to back neck edge. Adjust length of bands by adding or removing rows if necessary to make them fit smoothly. Bind off both bands and sew ends together.

Sew buttons to Left Front to correspond with buttonholes.

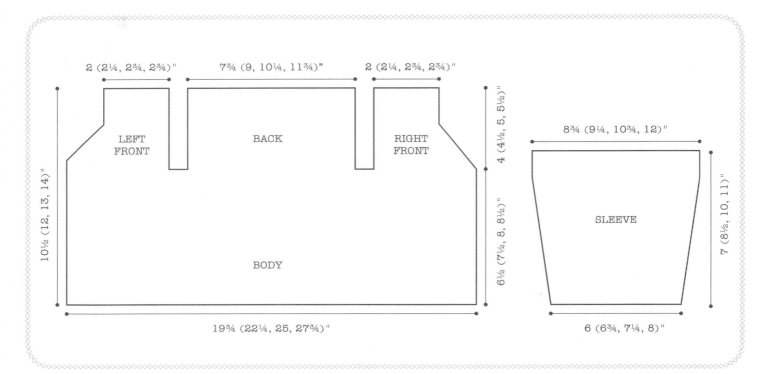

pattern stitch cardigan

Easy ✸ ✸ ✷ ✷

Sizes:

6 (12, 18, 24) months
Instructions are for size 6 months. Changes for sizes 12, 18 and 24 months are in parentheses.

Finished Measurements:
Chest: 21 (23, 25, 27)"
Length: 10½ (12, 13, 14)"

Materials:
* Worsted weight (4 medium) yarn, 3½ oz / 100g (approx 175 yds / 156m)
* Color A: 2 (2, 2, 2) skeins pink; approx. 200 (250, 300, 350) yds
* Color B: 1 skein ivory; approx. 20 (20, 25, 25) yds

* 2 medium stitch holders
* 1 button ¾" / 20mm

Needles:
* Size 9 / 5.5mm or size to obtain gauge
* Large eye yarn needle
* Crochet hook size I-9 / 5.5mm

Gauge:
16 sts & 26 rows = 4" / 10 cm in Seed st

Seed stitch:
Worked over an even number of stitches:
Row 1 (RS): * K1, p1; repeat from * to end.
Row 2 (WS): * P1, k1; repeat from * to end.

Body

With color A, cast on 88 (96, 104, 112) sts. Work in Seed Stitch until piece measures 6½ (7½, 8, 8½)", ending with a WS row.

DIVIDE FOR FRONTS AND BACK

Next row (RS): K23 (25, 27, 29) sts and place on a stitch holder for Right Front, bind off 4 sts for right armhole, k34 (38, 42, 46) sts and place on a stitch holder for Back, bind off 4 sts for left armhole, knit to end—23 (25, 27, 29) stitches remain for Left Front.

Left Front

Work even in Seed Stitch until armhole measures 2½ (3, 3½, 4)", ending with a RS row.

SHAPE NECK

Next row (WS): Bind off 7 (8, 9, 10), work in Seed Stitch to end—16 (17, 18, 19).
Next row (RS): Work in Seed Stitch to last 2 sts, k2tog.
Next row (WS): P2tog, work in Seed Stitch to end.
Repeat last 2 rows once more—12 (13, 14, 15) sts remain.

Work even in St st until piece measures 10½ (12, 13, 14)".
Bind off.

Back

With WS facing, slip Back sts from holder to needle and join yarn—34 (38, 42, 46) sts.
Beginning with a WS row, work in Seed Stitch until piece measures 10½ (12, 13, 14)".
Bind off.

Right Front

With WS facing, slip Right Front sts from holder to needle and join yarn.
Work even in Seed Stitch until armhole measures 2 (2½, 3, 3½)", ending with a WS row.
Next row – buttonhole row (RS): K1, p1, k1, yo, k2tog, work in Seed Stitch to end.
Work even in Seed Stitch until armhole measures 2½ (3, 3½, 4)", ending with a WS row.

SHAPE NECK

Next row (RS): Bind off 7 (8, 9, 10), work in Seed Stitch to end—16 (17, 18, 19).

Next row (WS): Work in Seed Stitch to last 2 sts, p2tog

Next row (RS): SSK, work in Seed Stitch to end.

Repeat last 2 rows once more—12 (13, 14, 15) sts remain.

Work even in St st until piece measures 10½ (12, 13, 14)". Bind off.

Sleeves (make 2)

With color A, cast on 24 (26, 28, 30) sts.

Work 3 rows in Seed Stitch.

Next row (RS): K1, kfb, work in Seed stitch to last 2 sts, kfb, p1—26 (28, 30, 32) sts.

Work 5 rows in Seed Stitch.

Repeat last 6 rows 4 (5, 6, 7) more times—34 (38, 42, 46) sts.

Work even in Seed Stitch until piece measures 7 (8½, 10, 11)". Bind off loosely.

Finishing

Sew shoulder seams. Sew sleeve seams, leaving ½" at top of sleeve open. Sew sleeves into armholes, sewing open section of sleeve seam to bound-off stitches at underarm.

EDGING

With crochet hook and color B, starting at left shoulder seam, work [sc1, ch1] along neck edge to corner, work [sc1, ch1, sc1] in the same space to turn corner, continue down left front to lower corner, work [sc1, ch1, sc1] at corner, continue across lower edge to right front corner, work [sc1, ch1, sc1] at corner, continue up right front to neck edge, work [sc1, ch1, sc1] at corner, continue around neck edge to start and fasten off. Sew button to Left Front to correspond with buttonhole.

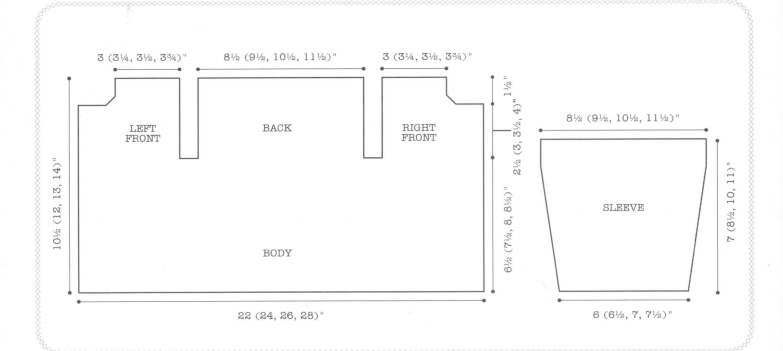

vests

"Not everyone thinks of vests for babies, but I love them. They are an easy way to add a bit of fun to the wardrobe while providing just the right amount of warmth. Vests are perfect for springtime over a dress or shirt, or layered under a cardigan for winter. They are great for little boys, and it's not always easy to find projects to make for the guys.

Both of the vests are worked in a chunky gauge, so they stitch up quickly. The basic vest is shown with the extra embellishment of duplicate stitch embroidery, but you can choose to leave it off for a pleasing one-color project. You could also add a second line of zigzags or put dots on the front. It's totally up to you.

The striped vest is worked in two colors for a classic look, but it would look amazing with each stripe in a different color. Or perhaps make the back with stripes and add some dots to the front. How about dots between the stripes? The possibilities are endless."

basic vest– blue zigzag

Intermediate ✹ ✹ ✹ ✵

Sizes:
6 (12, 18, 24) months
Instructions are for size 6 months. Changes for sizes 12, 18 and 24 months are in parentheses.

Finished Measurements:
Chest: 20 (22, 24, 26)"
Length: 11 (12, 13, 14)"

Materials:
* Worsted weight (④ medium) yarn, 3½ oz / 100g (approx 175 yds / 156m)
* Color A: 1 (1, 1, 1) skeins light blue; approx. 30 (40, 50, 60) yds
* Color B: 2 (2, 3, 3) skeins ivory; approx. 260 (300, 340, 380) yds
* 4 small stitch holders, 1 medium stitch holder

Needles:
* Size 11 / 8mm or size to obtain gauge for body
* Size 10½ / 6.5mm for edging
* Size 10½ / 6.5mm circular needle 16" long or set of double pointed needles for neck edging
* Large eye yarn needle

Gauge:
12 sts & 16 rows = 4" / 10 cm in St st using double strand of yarn and larger needles

K1 P1 Rib:
Worked over an even number of stitches:
Every Row: * K1, p1; repeat from * to end.

Notes:
Work with 2 strands of yarn held together throughout.

Back

With smaller needles and 2 strands of color A held together, cast on 32 (34, 38, 40) sts. Work 4 rows in K1 P1 Rib. Cut color A. Change to larger needles.
Change to 2 strands of color B held together and work even in St st until piece measures 7 (7½, 8, 8½)", ending with a WS row.

SHAPE ARMHOLES
Bind off 4 sts at the beginning of the next 2 rows.
Next row (RS): K1, ssk, knit to last 3 sts, k2tog, k1.
Next row (WS): Purl.
Repeat last 2 rows one more time—20 (22, 26, 28) sts remain.
Work even until piece measures 11 (12, 13, 14)", ending with a WS row.
Place first 4 (4, 5, 5) sts on a stitch holder for Right shoulder, place next 12 (14, 16, 18) sts on a stitch holder for back neck, place remaining 4 (4, 5, 5) sts on a stitch holder for Left shoulder.

Front
Work same as Back to armholes.

SHAPE ARMHOLES
Bind off 4 sts at the beginning of the next 2 rows.
Next row (RS): K1, ssk, knit to last 3 sts, k2tog, k1.
Next row (WS): Purl.
Repeat last 2 rows one more time—20 (22, 26, 28) sts remain.

SHAPE NECK
Row 1 (RS): K7 (8, 10, 11), k2tog, k1. Place remaining 10 (11, 13, 14) sts on holder.
Row 2 (WS): Purl.
Row 3: Knit to last 3 sts, k2tog, k1.
Row 4: Purl.
Repeat last 2 rows 4 (5, 6, 7) more times—4 (4, 5, 5) sts remain.
Work even until same length as back to shoulders. Place sts on a stitch holder for Left shoulder.
Re-join yarn to held stitches at center front—10 (11, 13, 14) sts.
Row 1 (RS): K1, ssk, knit to end.
Row 2 (WS): Purl.
Repeat last 2 rows 5 (6, 7, 8) more times—4 (4, 5, 5) sts remain.
Work even until same length as back to shoulders. Place sts on a stitch holder for Right shoulder.

Finishing

EMBROIDERY

Use 2 strands of color A held together to work zig-zag chart on front using duplicate stitch. Position bottom row of chart on Row 7 of front and back. Use 2 strands of color A held together to work dot chart on back using duplicate stitch. Place dots at random.

Join shoulder seams using 3-needle bind-off.

ARMBANDS

With smaller needles and 2 strands of color B held together, with RS facing, pick up and knit 40 (44, 48, 52) sts along armhole edge. Work 2 rows in K1 P1 Rib. Bind off in Rib.

Repeat for other armhole.
Sew side seams.

NECKBAND

Slip stitches from holder at back neck to circular or double pointed needles. With 2 strands of color B held together, knit these sts, then pick up and knit 14 (16, 18, 20) sts down Left neck edge, place marker, pick up and knit 1 st at center front, place marker, pick up and knit and 14 (16, 18, 20) sts up Right neck edge—41 (47, 53, 59) sts. Place marker and join to work in the round.

Next round: Work in K1 P1 Rib to 2 sts before marker, k2tog, purl center front stitch, ssk, work in K1 P1 Rib to end—39 (45, 51, 57) sts.
Repeat last round 2 more times.
Bind off loosely in Rib.

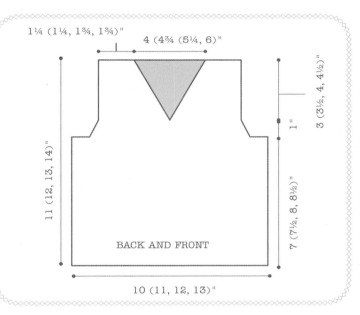

1¼ (1¼, 1¾, 1¾)"   4 (4¾ (5¼, 6)"
3 (3½, 4, 4½)"
1"
11 (12, 13, 14)"
7 (7½, 8, 8½)"

BACK AND FRONT

10 (11, 12, 13)"

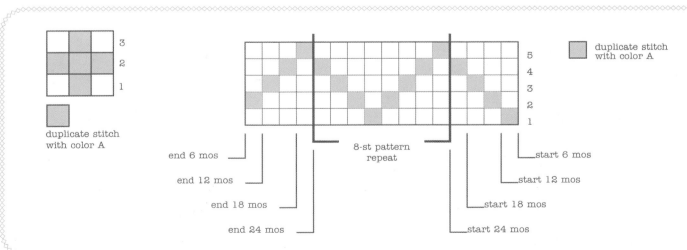

3
2
1

duplicate stitch
with color A

5
4
3
2
1

duplicate stitch
with color A

end 6 mos
end 12 mos
end 18 mos
end 24 mos

8-st pattern
repeat

start 6 mos
start 12 mos
start 18 mos
start 24 mos

basic vest—pink stripe

Sizes:
6 (12, 18, 24) months
Instructions are for size 6 months. Changes for sizes 12, 18 and 24 months are in parentheses.

Finished Measurements:
Chest: 20 (22, 24, 26)"
Length: 11 (12, 13, 14)"

Materials:
* Worsted weight (④ medium) yarn, 3½ oz / 100g (approx 175 yds / 156m)
* Color A: 1 (1, 2, 2) skeins ivory; approx. 140 (160, 190, 210) yds
* Color B: 1 (2, 2, 2) skeins pink; approx. 120 (140, 160, 180) yds
* 4 small stitch holders, 1 medium stitch holders

Needles:
* Size 11 / 8mm or size to obtain gauge for body
* Size 10½ / 6.5mm for edging
* Size 10½ / 6.5mm circular needle 16" long or set of double pointed needles for neck edging
* Large eye yarn needle

Gauge:
12 sts & 16 rows = 4" / 10 cm in St st using double strand of yarn and larger needles

K1 P1 Rib:
Worked over an even number of stitches:
Every Row: * K1, p1; repeat from * to end.

Notes:
Work with 2 strands of yarn held together throughout.
  Do not cut the yarn when changing colors. Carry the yarn not in use loosely up the side of the piece.

Back

With smaller needles and 2 strands of color A held together, cast on 32 (34, 38, 40) sts. Work 4 rows in K1 P1 Rib. Change to larger needles.
Change to 2 strands of color B held together and work 4 rows in St st. Change to color A and knit 4 rows in St st. Continue alternating 4 rows of color B with 4 rows of color A for remainder of piece.
Work in St st until piece measures 7 (7½, 8, 8½)", ending with a WS row.

SHAPE ARMHOLES
Bind off 4 sts at the beginning of the next 2 rows.
Next row (RS): K1, ssk, knit to last 3 sts, k2tog, k1.
Next row (WS): Purl.
Repeat last 2 rows one more time—20 (22, 26, 28) sts remain.
Work even until piece measures 11 (12, 13, 14)" , ending with a WS row.
Place first 4 (4, 5, 5) sts on a stitch holder for Right shoulder,
place next 12 (14, 16, 18) sts on a stitch holder for back neck, place remaining 4 (4, 5, 5) sts on a stitch holder for Left shoulder.

Front

Work same as Back to armholes.

SHAPE ARMHOLES
Bind off 4 sts at the beginning of the next 2 rows.
Next row (RS): K1, ssk, knit to last 3 sts, k2tog, k1.
Next row (WS): Purl.
Repeat last 2 rows one more time—20 (22, 26, 28) sts remain.

SHAPE NECK
Row 1 (RS): K7 (8, 10, 11), k2tog, k1. Place remaining 10 (11, 13, 14) sts on holder.
Row 2 (WS): Purl.
Row 3: Knit to last 3 sts, k2tog, k1.
Row 4: Purl.

Repeat last 2 rows 4 (5, 6, 7) more times—4 (4, 5, 5) sts remain.
Work even until same length as back to shoulders. Place sts on a stitch holder for Left shoulder.

Re-join yarn to held stitches at center front—10 (11, 13, 14) sts.

Row 1 (RS): K1, ssk, knit to end.

Row 2 (WS): Purl.

Repeat last 2 rows 5 (6, 7, 8) more times—4 (4, 5, 5) sts remain.
Work even until same length as back to shoulders. Place sts on a stitch holder for Right shoulder.

Finishing

Join shoulder seams using 3-needle bind-off.

ARMBANDS

With smaller needles and 2 strands of color A held together, with RS facing, pick up and knit 40 (44, 48, 52) sts along armhole edge. Work 2 rows in K1 P1 Rib. Bind off in Rib.
Repeat for other armhole.
Sew side seams.

NECKBAND

Slip stitches from holder at back neck to circular or double pointed needles. With 2 strands of color A held together, knit these sts, then pick up and knit 14 (16, 18, 20) sts down Left neck edge, place marker, pick up and knit 1 st at center front, place marker, pick up and knit and 14 (16, 18, 20) sts up Right neck edge—41 (47, 53, 59) sts. Place marker and join to work in the round.

Next round: Work in K1 P1 Rib to 2 sts before marker, k2tog, purl center front stitch, ssk, work in K1 P1 Rib to end—39 (45, 51, 57) sts.
Repeat last round 2 more times.
Bind off loosely in Rib.

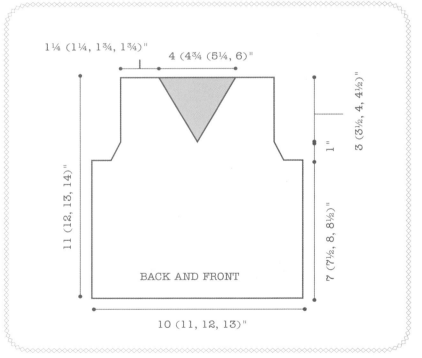

1¼ (1¼, 1¾, 1¾)"

4 (4¾ (5¼, 6)"

3 (3½, 4, 4½)"

11 (12, 13, 14)"

1"

7 (7½, 8, 8½)"

BACK AND FRONT

10 (11, 12, 13)"

blankets

"Every baby loves a blankie. In fact, some love them so much it's hard to tear them away long enough to wash them! My nephew was so attached to his blankie that my sister had to hang it on the clothesline after she washed it so he could sit under it and hold on.

Blankets are also one of the easiest projects to knit, since there is no shaping. This means you can add a colorful border or stripes and it will still be a quick and easy project.

All of the blankets in this section are worked in a chunky gauge. The borders are worked in garter stitch to prevent the edges from rolling and to add some nice texture. I have chosen to make the border in the basic blanket with a contrasting color, but you can easily work it in one color. Stripes in the other two blankets provide the opportunity to add color interest. You could even make the stripes more than one color.

Whichever blanket you choose, you will certainly make that special baby very happy."

pink border blanket

Sizes:
One size

Finished Measurements:
Width: 24"
Length: 28"

Materials:
* Bulky weight (**5** bulky) yarn, 3½ oz /100g (approx 120 yds / 109m)
* Color A: 2 skeins pink; approx 200 yds
* Color B: 4 skeins ivory; approx 400 yds
* 2 small and 1 large stitch holders

Needles:
* Size 13 / 8mm or size to obtain gauge
* Large eye yarn needle

Gauge:
10 sts & 12 rows = 4" / 10 cm in St st using double strand of yarn

Garter Stitch:
Knit every row.

Notes:
Work with 2 strands of yarn held together throughout.

Blanket

With 2 strands of color A held together, cast on 64 sts. Knit 8 rows.

Next row (RS): K6 and place these 6 sts on a stitch holder, change to 2 strands of color B held together and k52, place remaining 6 sts on a stitch holder.

Beginning with a purl row, work in St st with color B on remaining 52 sts until piece measures 25", ending with a WS row. Place sts on a stitch holder.

Slip border sts from holder at left side to needle. Work in Garter st with color A until border is the same length as center panel of blanket, ending with a WS row. Place sts back on holder.

Slip border sts from holder at right side to needle. Work in Garter st with color A until border is the same length as center panel of blanket, ending with a WS row.

Next row (RS): With color A, knit border stitches, knit across 52 center panel stitches from holder, knit left border stitches from holder—64 sts.

Knit 7 rows. Bind off.

Sew side borders to sides of center panel.

blue striped blanket

Easy ✳ ✳ ✲ ✲

Sizes:
One size

Finished Measurements:
Width: 25"
Length: 30"

Materials:
* Super Bulky ((6) super bulky) yarn,
* 6 oz / 170g (approx 106 yds / 97m)
* Color A: 3 skeins light blue; approx 318 yds
* Color B: 3 skeins ivory; approx 318 yds

* 2 small and 1 large stitch holders

Needles:
* Size 13 / 9mm or size to obtain gauge
* Large eye yarn needle

Gauge:
10 sts & 12 rows = 4" / 10 cm in St st

Notes:
Do not cut the yarn when changing colors. Carry the yarn not in use loosely up the side of the piece.

Blanket

With color A, cast on 58 sts. Knit 4 rows.

Next row (RS): K4 and place these 4 sts on a stitch holder, change to color B and k50, plae remaining 4 sts on a stitch holder.

Beginning with a purl row, work 3 rows in St st on remaining 50 sts.

Continuing in St st, alternate 2 rows of color A with 4 rows of color B until there are 12 color B stripes.

Cut color B. Place sts on a stitch holder

Slip border sts from holder at left side to needle. Work in Garter st with color A until border is the same length as center panel of blanket, ending with a WS row. Place sts back on holder.

Slip border sts from holder at right side to needle. Work in Garter st with color A until border is the same length as center panel of blanket, ending with a WS row.

Next row (RS): With color A, knit border stitches, knit across 50 center panel stitches from holder, knit left border stitches from holder—58 sts.

Knit 4 rows. Bind off.

Sew side borders to sides of center panel.

green striped blanket

Easy ✸ ✸ ✸ ✸ ✸

Sizes:
One size

Finished Measurements:
Width: 24"
Length: 28"

Materials:
* Worsted weight (④ medium) yarn,
  3½ oz / 100g (approx 175 yds / 156m)
* Color A: 2 skeins light green; approx 300 yds
* Color B: 2 skeins ivory; approx 340 yds

Needles:
* Size 11 / 8mm or size to obtain gauge

Gauge:
12 sts & 16 rows = 4" / 10 cm in St st using
double strand of yarn

Notes:
Work with 2 strands of yarn held together throughout.
   Do not cut the yarn when changing colors. Carry
the yarn not in use loosely up the side of the piece.

Blanket

With 2 strands of color A held together, cast on 72 sts.
Knit 6 rows.
Change to 2 strands of color B held together.
Next row (RS): Knit.
Next row (WS): K5, p62, k5.
Repeat last 2 rows one more time.
Maintaining center of blanket in St st, with 5 stitch borders on
either side as set, change colors as follows:
* 2 rows A.
6 rows B.
4 rows A.
2 rows B.
4 rows A.
6 rows B.
2 rows A.
4 rows B.
Repeat from * 2 more times.
2 rows A.
4 rows B. Cut color B.
Knit 6 rows with A. Bind off.

hats

"Keeping babies' heads warm is important, even if they don't always agree with you. Since hats are something a mother can never have enough of, feel free to make them in every color.

The basic hat couldn't be easier or faster. It's knit using two needles instead of in the round. Just sew up the back seam and you're ready to go. I've included the option of knitting little ears for the hat to add a little fun and whimsy.

The second hat is worked in two colors, starting with the ribbed band and then adding duplicate stitch when the knitting is finished. This is a perfect project for adding your own touch by varying the colors or using several colors, one for the rib and another for the duplicate stitch."

hat with ears

Easy

Sizes:
One size

Finished Measurements:
Head circumference: 16"

Materials:
* Worsted weight ((4) medium) yarn,
  3½ oz /100g (approx 175 yds /156m)
* Color A: 1 skein blue; approx. 75 yds
* Color B: 1 skein ivory; approx. 15 yds

Needles:
* Size 11 / 8mm or size to obtain gauge
* Large eye yarn needle

Gauge:
12 sts & 16 rows = 4" / 10 cm in St st using
double strand of yarn and larger needles

K1 P1 Rib:
Worked over an even number of stitches:
Every row: * K1, p1; repeat from * to end.

HAT

With 2 strands of color A held together, cast on 50 sts.
Work in K1 P1 Rib for 9 rows.
Change to St st and work until piece measures 4", ending with
a WS row.

SHAPE CROWN

Row 1 (RS): * K2tog, k3; repeat from * to end—40 sts.
Row 2 and all WS rows: Purl.
Row 3: * K2tog, k3; repeat from * to end—32 sts.
Row 5: * K2tog, k2; repeat from * to end—24 sts.
Row 7: * K2tog, k1, repeat from * to end—16 sts.
Row 9: K2tog to end—8 sts.
Cut yarn. Use yarn needle to pull ends through remaining 8
sts, pull tight and fasten off.

EARS – MAKE 2 WITH COLOR A AND 2 WITH COLOR B

With 2 strands of yarn held together, cast on 6 sts.
Rows 1-4: Knit.
Row 5: K1, k2tog twice, k1—4 sts.
Row 6: Knit.
Row 7: K2tog twice—2 sts.
Bind off.

Join one ear of color A to one ear of color B, sewing around
outer edges.

Finishing

Sew seam. Sew ears onto hat with color B side facing front.

hat-pink trim

Easy ✹ ✹ ✵ ✵

Sizes:
One size

Finished Measurements:
Head circumference: 16"

Materials:
* Worsted weight (④ medium) yarn,
  3½ oz / 100g (approx 175 yds / 156m)
* Color A: 1 skein ivory; approx. 75 yds
* Color B: 1 skein pink; approx. 15 yds

Needles:
* Size 11 / 8mm or size to obtain gauge
* Large eye yarn needle

Gauge:
12 sts & 16 rows = 4" / 10 cm in St st using
double strand of yarn and larger needles

K1 P1 Rib:
Worked over an even number of stitches:
Every row: * K1, p1; repeat from * to end.

HAT
With 2 strands of color A held together, cast on 50 sts.
Change to 2 strands of color B held together.
Work 1 row K1 P1 Rib.
Change to 2 strands of color A held together.
Work 1 row K1 P1 Rib.
Change to 2 strands of color B held together.
Work 1 row K1 P1 Rib.
Change to 2 strands of A held together and work in St st until
piece measures 4", ending with a WS row.

SHAPE CROWN
Row 1 (RS): * K2tog, k3; repeat from * to end—40 sts.
Row 2 and all WS rows: Purl.
Row 3: * K2tog, k3; repeat from * to end—32 sts.
Row 5: * K2tog, k2; repeat from * to end—24 sts.
Row 7: * K2tog, k1, repeat from * to end—16 sts.
Row 9: K2tog to end—8 sts.
Cut yarn. Use yarn needle to pull ends through remaining
8 sts, pull tight and fasten off.

Finishing

EMBROIDERY
Use 2 strands of color B held together to work dot chart
around hat. Position bottom row of chart on Row 2 of St st.

Sew seam.

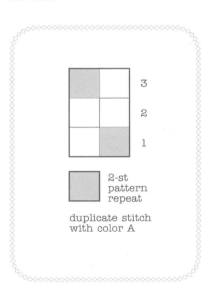

duplicate stitch
with color A

booties

"There is nothing cuter than a baby's tiny feet, and I have always loved making booties to keep them warm and toasty. Booties are also one of those projects that are great for a baby shower because they work up fast, you can make them in any color, and they are something every baby needs. Hand knit booties will have them oohing and aahing!

The three different booties are each knit on two needles for ease and speed. The blue booties are worked in one color to the ribbed top; then a second color is added in. Work the entire bootie in a single color if you prefer.

The pink booties are knit with a contrasting sole, with garter stitch in stripes at the top echoing the contrasting color. Lastly, the green booties have a contrasting sole and short, striped ribbing at the top.

Make one or make them all. They are the perfect way to keep those tiny tootsies warm."

blue booties

Sizes:
One size

Finished Measurements:
Foot length: 4"

Materials:
* Worsted weight (④ medium) yarn,
  3½ oz / 100g (approx 175 yds / 156m)
* Color A: 1 skein light blue; approx. 60 yds
* Color B: 1 skein ivory; approx. 5 yds

Needles:
* Size 7 / 4.5mm or size to obtain gauge

* Large eye yarn needle

Gauge:
17 sts & 24 rows = 4" / 10 cm in St st using
double strand of yarn and larger needles

K1 P1 Rib:
Worked over an odd number of stitches:
Row 1 (RS): P1, * k1, p1; repeat from * to end.
Row 2 (WS): K1, * p1, k1; repeat from to end.

Notes:
While working the striped cuff, do not cut the yarn
when changing colors. Carry the yarn not in use
loosely up the side of the piece.

SOLE
With color A, cast on 26 sts.
Row 1 (RS): Knit.
Row 2 (WS): K1, yo, k11, [yo, k1] twice, yo, k11, yo, k1—31 sts.
Rows 3, 5, 7 and 9: Knit, working each yarn over through the back loop.
Row 4: K2, yo, k11, yo, k2, yo, k3, yo, k11, yo, k2—36 sts.
Row 6: K3, yo, k11, [yo, k4] twice, yo, k11, yo, k3—41 sts.
Row 8: Knit.

SIDES
Starting with a RS row, work 4 rows in St st.

INSTEP
Row 1 (RS): K23, ssk, turn work. 16 sts remain unworked.
Row 2 (WS): Sl 1, p5, p2tog, turn work.

Row 3: Sl 1, k5, ssk, turn work.
Rows 4-12: Repeat Rows 2 and 3 four more times, then work Row 2 once more—29 sts.
Row 13 (RS): Sl 1, k5, ssk, knit to end of row.
Row 14: P16, p2tog, purl to end of row—27 sts.

CUFF
Work in K1 P1 Rib for 1½".
Change to color B. Work 2 rows in Rib.
Change to color A. Work 2 rows in Rib.
Change to color B. Work 1 row in Rib. Bind off.

Finishing
Sew sole seam and center back seam.

pink booties

Easy ✳ ✳ ✵ ✵

Sizes:
One size

Finished Measurements:
Foot length: 4"

Materials:
* Worsted weight (④ medium) yarn, 3½ oz /100g (approx 175 yds / 156m)
* Color A: 1 skein pink; approx. 30 yds
* Color B: 1 skein ivory; approx. 30 yds

Needles:
* Size 7 / 4.5mm or size to obtain gauge
* Large eye yarn needle

Gauge:
17 sts & 24 rows = 4" / 10 cm in St st using double strand of yarn and larger needles

K1 P1 Rib:
Worked over an odd number of stitches:
Row 1 (RS): P1, * k1, p1; repeat from * to end.
Row 2 (WS): K1, * p1, k1; repeat from to end.

Garter Stitch:
Knit every row.

Notes:
While working the striped cuff, do not cut the yarn when changing colors. Carry the yarn not in use loosely up the side of the piece.

SOLE
With color A, cast on 26 sts.
Row 1 (RS): Knit.
Row 2 (WS—): K1, yo, k11, [yo, k1] twice, yo, k11, yo, k1—31 sts.
Rows 3, 5, 7 and 9: Knit, working each yarn over through the back loop.
Row 4: K2, yo, k11, yo, k2, yo, k3, yo, k11, yo, k2—36 sts.
Row 6: K3, yo, k11, [yo, k4] twice, yo, k11, yo, k3—41 sts.
Row 8: Knit.

SIDES
Change to color B. Starting with a RS row, work 4 rows in St st.

INSTEP
Row 1 (RS): K23, ssk, turn work. 16 sts remain unworked.
Row 2 (WS): Sl 1, p5, p2tog, turn work.
Row 3: Sl 1, k5, ssk, turn work.
Rows 4-12: Repeat Rows 2 and 3 four more times, then work Row 2 once more—29 sts.
Row 13 (RS): Sl 1, k5, ssk, knit to end of row.
Row 14: P16, p2tog, purl to end of row—27 sts.

CUFF
Work 2 rows in K1 P1 Rib.
Change to color A. Knit 2 rows.
Change to color B. Knit 2 rows.
Change to color A. Knit 2 rows.
Change to color B. Knit 1 row. Bind off.

Finishing
Sew sole seam and center back seam.

green booties

Easy ✹ ✹ ✵ ✵

Sizes:
One size

Finished Measurements:
Foot length: 4"

Materials:
* Worsted weight (④ medium) yarn, 3½ oz / 100g (approx 175 yds / 156m)
* Color A: 1 skein light green; approx. 30 yds
* Color B: 1 skein ivory; approx. 30 yds

Needles:
* Size 7 / 4.5mm or size to obtain gauge
* Large eye yarn needle

Gauge:
17 sts & 24 rows = 4" / 10 cm in St st using double strand of yarn and larger needles

K1 P1 Rib:
Worked over an odd number of stitches:
Row 1 (RS): P1, * k1, p1; repeat from * to end.
Row 2 (WS): K1, * p1, k1; repeat from to end.

Notes:
While working the striped cuff, do not cut the yarn when changing colors. Carry the yarn not in use loosely up the side of the piece.

SOLE
With color A, cast on 26 sts.
Row 1 (RS): Knit.
Row 2 (WS): K1, yo, k11, [yo, k1] twice, yo, k11, yo, k1—31 sts.
Rows 3, 5, 7 and 9: Knit, working each yarn over through the back loop.
Row 4: K2, yo, k11, yo, k2, yo, k3, yo, k11, yo, k2—36 sts.
Row 6: K3, yo, k11, [yo, k4] twice, yo, k11, yo, k3—41 sts.
Row 8: Knit.

SIDES
Change to color B. Starting with a RS row, work 4 rows in St st.

INSTEP
Row 1 (RS): K23, ssk, turn work. 16 sts remain unworked.
Row 2 (WS): Sl 1, p5, p2tog, turn work.

Row 3: Sl 1, k5, ssk, turn work.
Rows 4-12: Repeat Rows 2 and 3 four more times, then work Row 2 once more—29 sts.
Row 13 (RS): Sl 1, k5, ssk, knit to end of row.
Row 14: P16, p2tog, purl to end of row—27 sts.

CUFF
Work 2 rows in K1 P1 Rib.
Change to color A. Work 2 rows in Rib.
Change to color B. Work 2 rows in Rib.
Change to color A. Work 2 rows in Rib.
Change to color B. Work 1 row in Rib. Bind off.

Finishing
Sew sole seam and center back seam.

✳ mitts ✳

"What could be sweeter than baby mitts? They are the perfect solution for keeping little ones' tiny fingers warm, and hopefully out of trouble. Mitts are fun to knit and work up in a jiffy on two needles. I've included a pair of fingerless mitts for when Baby gets a little older and wants to be able to pick up and play with toys.

The basic mitt pattern is worked in two colors, either with one bold stripe at the top or narrower stripes as you go. For an unmatched pair, you might want to vary the colors or reverse the colors on each mitt.

Fingerless mitts provide warmth for the baby, but allow the use of those curious little fingers. They are also just as cute as can be. These mitts are worked in two colors with a little duplicate stitch detail."

mitts

Sizes:
One size

Finished Measurements:
Length: 4"

Materials:
* Worsted weight (④ medium) yarn,
  3½ oz / 100g (approx 175 yds / 156m)
* Color A: 1 skein ivory; approx. 30 yds
* Color B: 1 skein contrasting color; approx.
  30 yds

Needles:
* Size 7 / 4.5mm or size to obtain gauge
* Large eye yarn needle
* Crochet hook size H-8 / 5mm

Gauge:
16 sts & 32 rows = 4" / 10 cm in Garter st
using a single strand of yarn

K1 P1 Rib:
Worked over an odd number of stitches:
Row 1 (RS): P1, * k1, p1; repeat from * to end.
Row 2 (WS): K1, * p1, k1; repeat from to end.

Garter stitch:
Knit every row.

Notes:
While working stripes, do not cut the yarn when
changing colors. Carry the yarn not in use loosely up
the side of the piece.

CUFF
Cast on 24 sts.
Work 7 rows K1 P1 Rib.

HAND
Work 20 rows in Garter stitch.

Shape tip
Row 1 (RS): * K2tog, k1; repeat from * to end—16 sts.
Row 2 and all WS rows: Knit.
Row 3: K1, * k2tog, k1; repeat from * to end—11 sts.
Row 5: K1, * k2tog; repeat from * to end—6 sts.
Bind off.

Repeat for other hand.

Finishing
Sew side and tip seams.

CORD
Using crochet hook, make chain 14" long. Attach one end of
cord to each mitt.

Variations

GREEN TIPPED MITTS
Use ivory for cuff and first 14 rows of Garter stitch. Change to
green for remainder of mitt. Use ivory for cord.

BLUE STRIPED MITTS
Cast on and work first row of rib with blue. Work 6 rows of rib
with ivory. For Garter stitch, alternate 4 rows of ivory with 2
rows of blue. Use blue for cord.

fingerless mitts

Easy

Sizes:
One size

Finished Measurements:
Length: 3½"

Materials:
* Worsted weight (4 medium) yarn,
  3½ oz / 100g (approx 175 yds / 156m)
* Color A: 1 skein pink; approx. 10 yds
* Color B: 1 skein ivory; approx. 25 yds

Needles:
* Size 7 / 4.5mm or size to obtain gauge
* Large eye yarn needle

Gauge:
16 sts & 24 rows = 4" / 10 cm in Stockinette st
using a single strand of yarn

K1 P1 Rib:
Worked over an odd number of stitches:
Row 1 (RS): P1, * k1, p1; repeat from * to end.
Row 2 (WS): K1, * p1, k1; repeat from to end.

CUFF
With color A, cast on 25 sts.
Work 1 row K1 P1 Rib.
Change to color B.
Work 5 rows K1 P1 Rib.
Change to Stockinette st and work even until piece
measures 3".
Change to color A and knit 2 rows.
Bind off.

Finishing

EMBROIDERY

Use color A to work zig-zag chart around cuff. Position bottom row of chart on Row 2 of Stockinette st.

Sew side seam from cast-on edge to top of ribbing. Leave 1" open for thumb hole. Sew remainder of side seam to bound-off edge.

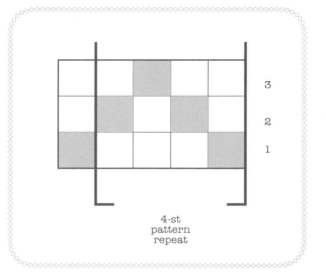

3

2

1

4-st
pattern
repeat

✳ extras for baby ✳

"Now that we've covered the basics for Baby to wear and bundle up, it's time to add a few 'extras.'

First up are the bibs. Worked in basic garter stitch and simple stripes, you'll be able to knit them up in a few hours. They are made in a machine washable yarn, so you can keep Baby clean without worrying about what gets spilled.

Soft and just the right size for little fingers, the blocks are colorful and have fun letters to play with. You can spell out several words for Baby with just the three letters provided.

Little sweaters and clothes can be tricky on hangers and can easily come tumbling off. These hanger covers are great for keeping baby garments on the hanger. They are worked without shaping, and range from easy stripes to intermediate color changes.

Washcloths are the perfect last-minute gift for Baby. Knit in cotton, they are soft and absorbent and can be made in very little time. There are two different patterns and several colorways to choose from."

bibs

Easy ✹ ✹ ✦ ✦

Sizes:
One size

Finished Measurements:
Width: 8"
Length: 8"

Materials:
* Worsted weight (④ medium) washable yarn,
  2½ oz / 70g (approx 120 yds / 109m)
* Color A: 1 skein ivory; approx. 60 yds
* Color B: 1 skein blue or green; approx. 60 yds

* 1 small stitch holder
* 1 button 1" / 25mm

Needles:
* Size 9 / 5.5mm or size to obtain gauge
* Large eye yarn needle

Gauge:
16 sts & 30 rows = 4" / 10 cm in Garter st

Notes:
Do not cut the yarn when changing colors. Carry the yarn not in use loosely up the side of the piece.

Blue Bib

With color A, cast on 32 sts.
*Knit 8 rows. Change to color B. Knit 8 rows. Change to color A. Repeat from * 2 more times. Cut color B.
With color A, knit 8 rows.

STRAPS

Next row (RS): K7 and place these stitches on a holder. Bind off center 18 sts, knit to end. 7 sts remain.
Work even in Garter st until strap measures 4".
Next row – buttonhole row (RS): K3, yo, k2tog, k2.
Knit 3 rows.
Bind off.
Return held sts to needle and rejoin color A.
Knit even until strap measures 4½". Bind off.

FINISHING

Sew button to strap opposite buttonhole.

Green Bib

With color A, cast on 32 sts.
*Knit 4 rows. Change to color B. Knit 2 rows. Change to color A. Repeat from * 7 more times. Cut color B.
With color A, knit 4 rows.

STRAPS

Next row (RS): K7 and place these stitches on a holder. Bind off center 18 sts, knit to end. 7 sts remain.
Work even in Garter st until strap measures 4".
Next row – buttonhole row (RS): K3, yo, k2tog, k2.
Knit 3 rows.
Bind off.
Return held sts to needle and join color B.
Knit even until strap measures 4½". Bind off.

FINISHING

Sew button to strap opposite buttonhole.

blocks

Easy

Sizes:
One size

Finished Measurements:
Approx. 3" x 3" x 3"

Materials:
* Worsted weight (**4** medium) yarn,
  3½ oz / 100g (approx 175 yds / 156m)

* Odds and ends of 6 different colors: Ivory,
  light blue, dark blue, pink, magenta and green.
* 3" cube upholstery foam

Needles:
* Size 8 / 5mm or size to obtain gauge
* Large eye yarn needle

Gauge:
16 sts & 24 rows = 4" / 10 cm in Garter stitch
using a single strand of yarn

Multi Stripe Side

With ivory, cast on 12 sts.
Working in Stockinette st throughout, * work 1 row dark blue, 1
row light blue, 1 row green, 1 row pink, 1 row magenta and
1 row ivory. Repeat from * 2 more times. Bind off.

Seed Stitch Side

With ivory, cast on 12 sts.
Row 1 (RS): * K1, p1; repeat from * to end.
Row 2 (WS): * P1, k1; repeat from * to end.
Repeat these 2 rows 7 more times. Bind off.

Garter Stitch Side

With green, cast on 12 sts.
Knit 24 rows. Bind off.

Dot Side

With light blue, cast on 12 sts.
Work 15 rows in Stockinette st. Bind off.
With dark blue, work dot pattern from chart using duplicate
stitch embroidery.

Vertical Stripe Side

With pink, cast on 14 sts.
Work 16 rows Stockinette st. Bind off.
With ivory, work duplicate stitch embroidery stripes along every third column of stitches—4 stripes made.

Letter Side

With magenta, cast on 13 sts.
Work 16 rows Stockinette st. Bind off.
With ivory, work desired letter from chart using duplicate stitch embroidery.

Sew sides together, inserting foam before closing up last side.

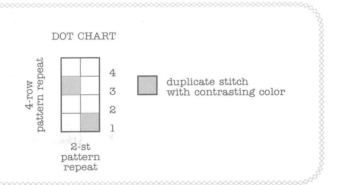

DOT CHART

4-row pattern repeat

4
3
2
1

duplicate stitch with contrasting color

2-st pattern repeat

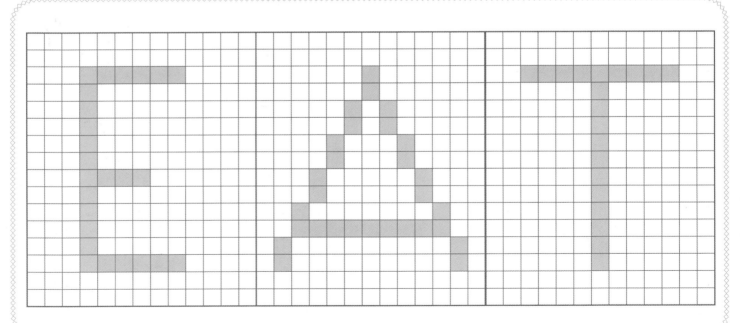

hanger covers

Easy

Sizes:
One size

Finished Measurements:
To fit hanger 10" long

Materials:
* Worsted weight (4 medium) yarn, 3½ oz / 100g (approx 175 yds / 156m)
* Striped cover: 1 skein each of green, ivory, pink and blue; approx 20 yds each
* Checkerboard cover: 1 skein each of ivory and green; approx. 40 yds each
* Dot cover: 1 skein each of ivory and pink; approx 40 yds each

Needles:
* Size 8 / 5mm or size to obtain gauge
* Large eye yarn needle

Gauge:
16 sts & 24 rows = 4" / 10 cm in Stockinette st using a single strand of yarn

Striped cover

With green, cast on 42 sts.
Working in Stockinette st throughout, * work 2 rows green, o2 rows ivory, 2 rows pink and 2 rows blue. Repeat from * 2 more times. Bind off.
Fold cover in half with purl side of work to outside and sew in place around hanger.

Checkerboard Cover

NOTE: 2 colors are used on each row. Carry the color not in use loosely across the WS of the work.
With ivory, cast on 40 sts.
Row 1 (RS): * K2 with ivory, k2 with green; repeat from * to end.
Row 2 (WS): * P2 with green, p2 with ivory; repeat from * to end.
Row 3: * K2 with green, k2 with ivory; repeat from * to end.
Row 4: * P2 with ivory, p2 with green; repeat form * to end.
Repeat these 4 rows 5 more times. Bind off.
Fold cover in half and sew in place around hanger.

Dot Cover

NOTE: 2 colors are used on each row. Carry the color not in use loosely across the WS of the work.
With ivory, cast on 44 sts.
Row 1 (WS): With ivory, purl.
Row 2 (RS): * K3 with ivory, k1 with pink; repeat from * to end.
Row 3: P2 with ivory, * p1 with pink, p3 with ivory; repeat from * to last 2 sts, p1 with pink, p1 with ivory.
Repeat the last 2 rows 10 more times. Bind off.
Fold cover in half and sew in place around hanger.

washcloths

Easy ✴ ✴ ✴ ✴

Sizes:
One size

Finished Measurements:
8"x10"

Materials:
* Worsted weight (❹ medium) cotton yarn, 2½ oz / 70g (approx 120 yds / 109m)
* Color A: 1 skein ivory; approx. 60 yds
* Color B: 1 skein contrasting color; yardage varies

Needles:
* Size 8 / 5mm or size to obtain gaug

Gauge:
15 sts & 30 rows = 4" / 10 cm in Garter st

Notes:
Do not cut the yarn when changing colors. Carry the yarn not in use loosely up the side of the piece.

Blue Washcloth

With color A, cast on 41 sts.
Rows 1-5: With A, knit.
Row 6: With A, purl.
Rows 7 and 8: With B, knit.

Row 9: With A, knit.
Row 10: With A, purl.
Repeat these 10 rows 4 more times, then work Rows 1-4 again. Bind off.

Multi-color Washcloth

With color A, cast on 41 sts.

Rows 1-5: With A, knit.

Row 6: With A, purl.

Rows 7 and 8: With blue, knit.

Row 9: With A, knit.

Row 10: With A, purl.

Repeat these 10 rows 4 more times, but work Rows 7 and 8 with pink, then with green, then with blue, then with pink.

Work Rows 1-4 again.

Bind off.

Pink Diagonal Washcloth

Stripe Pattern: 2 rows pink, 4 rows ivory.

With pink, cast on 5.

Begin Stripe Pattern.

Row 1: Knit.

Row 2: K2, yo, knit to end.

Maintaining Stripe Pattern throughout, repeat Row 2 until there are 59 sts.

Next row: K2, yo, k2tog twice, knit to end.

Maintaining Stripe pattern throughout, repeat last row until there are 5 sts.

Knit 1 row.

Bind off.

knit in a day

Abbreviations List

ch	chain
k	knit
kfb	knit in the front and the back of the next stitch
k2tog	knit 2 stitches together
p	purl
p2tog	purl 2 stitches together
RS	Right Side
sc	single crochet
sl	slip next stitch as if to purl
ssk	slip, slip, knit – slip 2 stitches separately as if to knit, slip them together back to the left needle, then knit them together through the back loops
st(s)	stitch(es)
St st	Stockinette stitch – knit the right side rows, purl the wrong side rows
WS	Wrong Side
yo	yarn over

general instructions

Skill Levels for Knitting

Beginner — Projects for first-time knitters using basic knit and purl stitches. Minimal shaping.

Easy — Projects using basic stitches, repetitive stitch patterns, simple color changes, and simple shaping and finishing.

Intermediate — Projects with a variety of stitches, such as basic cables and lace, simple intarsia, double-pointed needles and knitting in the round needle techniques, mid-level shaping and finishing.

Experienced — Projects using advanced techniques and stitches, such as short rows, fair isle, more intricate intarsia, cables, lace patterns, and numerous color changes.

Yarn Weight Symbol & Category Names	0 Lace	1 Super Fine	2 Fine	3 Light	4 Medium	5 Bulky	6 Super Bulky
Types of Yarns in Category	Fingering 10-count crochet thread	Sock, Fingering, Baby	Sport, Baby	DK, Light Worsted	Worsted, Afghan, Aran	Chunky, Craft, Rug	Bulky, Roving
Knit Gauge Range in Stockinette Stitch to 4"	33 – 40 sts	27 – 32 sts	23 – 26 sts	21 – 24 st	16 – 20 sts	12 – 15 sts	6 – 11 sts
Recommended Needle in Metric Size Range	1.5 – 2.25 mm	2.25 – 3.25 mm	3.25 – 3.75 mm	3.75 – 4.5 mm	4.5 – 5.5 mm	5.5 – 8 mm	8 mm and larger
Recommended Needle U.S. Size Range	000 – 1	1 to 3	3 to 5	5 to 7	7 to 9	9 to 11	11 and larger

general instructions

Yarn Equivalents

PG 10: GREEN & WHITE PULLOVER
Patons Canadiana: 3 ½ oz/100g, 205yds/187m, White #10005 & Cherished Green #10230

PG 15: BASIC PULLOVER – GRAY TRIM
Lion Brand Wool-Ease: 3oz/85g, 197 yds/180m, Grey Heather #151 & Fisherman #99

PG 19: BASIC PULLOVER – PINK DOTS
Lion Brand Wool-Ease: 3oz/85g, 197 yds/180m, Fisherman #99 & Raspberry #166

PG 24: GREEN & WHITE CARDIGAN
Patons Canadiana: 3 ½ oz/100g, 205yds/187m, White #10005 & Cherished Green #10230

PG 29: TWO COLOR CARDIGAN
Lion Brand Vanna's Choice: 3 ½ oz/100g, 170 yds/156m, White #100 & Silver Blue #105

PG 33: PATTERN STITCH CARDIGAN
Lion Brand Wool-Ease: 3oz/85g, 197 yds/180m, Blossom #165

PG 38: BASIC VEST – BLUE ZIG ZAG
Lion Brand Vanna's Choice: 3 ½ oz/100g, 170 yds/156m, White #100 & Silver Blue #105

PG 43: BASIC VEST – PINK STRIPE
Patons Canadiana: 3 ½ oz/100g, 205yds/187m, White #10005 & Cherished Pink #10420

PG 48: PINK BORDER BLANKET
Patons Beehive Baby Chunky: 3 ½ oz/100g, 120yds/109m, White #05 & Puffy Pink #420

PG 51: BLUE STRIPED BLANKET
Lion Brand Wool-Ease Thick & Quick: 6oz/170g, 106 yds/97 m, Fisherman #99 & Glacier #105

PG 52: GREEN STRIPED BLANKET
Patons Canadiana: 3 ½ oz/100g, 205yds/187m, White #10005 & Cherished Green #10230

PG 56: HAT WITH EARS
Lion Brand Vanna's Choice: 3 ½ oz/100g, 170 yds/156m, White #100 & Silver Blue #105

PG 59: HAT – PINK TRIM
Lion Brand Vanna's Choice: 3 ½ oz/100g, 170 yds/156m, White #100 & Dusty Rose #140

PG 62: BLUE BOOTIES
Patons Canadiana: 3 ½ oz/100g, 205yds/187m, White #10005 & Pale Water Blue #10143

PG 65: PINK BOOTIES
Patons Canadiana: 3 ½ oz/100g, 205yds/187m, White #10005 & Cherished Pink #10420

PG 66: GREEN BOOTIES
Patons Canadiana: 3 ½ oz/100g, 205yds/187m, White #10005 & Cherished Green #10230

PG 70: MITTS
Green: Patons Canadiana: 3 ½ oz/100g, 205yds/187m, White #10005 & Cherished Green #10230
Blue: Lion Brand Vanna's Choice: 3 ½ oz/100g, 170 yds/156m, White #100 & Silver Blue #105

PG 73: FINGERLESS MITTS
Lion Brand Vanna's Choice: 3 ½ oz/100g, 170 yds/156m, White #100 & Dusty Rose #140

PG 78: BIBS
Blue: Patons Canadiana: 3 ½ oz/100g, 205yds/187m, White #10005 & Pale Water Blue #10143
Green: Patons Canadiana: 3 ½ oz/100g, 205yds/187m, White #10005 & Cherished Green #10230

PG 81: BLOCKS
Lion Brand Wool-Ease: 3oz/85g, 197 yds/180m, Fisherman #99, Zinnia #196, Blossom #165, Indigo #118
Lion Brand Vanna's Choice Baby: 3 ½ oz/100g, 170 yds/156m, Sweet Pea #169
Lion Brand Vanna's Choice: 3 ½ oz/100g, 170 yds/156m, Silver Blue #105

PG 85: HANGER COVERS
Lion Brand Vanna's Choice Baby: 3 ½ oz/100g, 170 yds/156m, Sweet Pea #169 & Lamb #98
Lion Brand Vanna's Choice: 3 ½ oz/100g, 170 yds/156m, Silver Blue #105 & Dusty Rose #140

PG 86: WASHCLOTH
Lily Sugar & Cream: 2 ½ oz/70g, 120 yds/90m, Ecru #4, Light Blue #26, Tea Rose #42 & Country Green #1222

Duplicate Stitch

Duplicate Stitch is worked on Stockinette Stitch. Each knit stitch forms a V and you want to completely cover that V, so that the design appears to have been knit into the sweater. Each square on a chart represents one knit stitch that is to be covered by a Duplicate Stitch.

Thread a tapestry/yarn needle with an 18" (45.5 cm) length of embroidery floss/yarn. Beginning at lower right of a design and with right side facing, bring the needle up from the wrong side at the base of the V, leaving an end to be woven in later (never tie knots). The needle should always go between the strands of yarn. Follow the right side of the V up and insert the needle from right to left under the legs of the V immediately above it, keeping the floss/yarn on top of the stitch (Fig. 1), and draw through. Follow the left side of the V back down to the base and insert the needle back through the bottom of the same stitch where the first stitch began (Fig. 2, Duplicate Stitch completed).

Continuing to follow chart, bring needle up through the next stitch. Repeat for each stitch, keeping tension even with tension of knit fabric to avoid puckering.

When a length of floss/yarn is finished, run it under several stitches on back of work to secure.

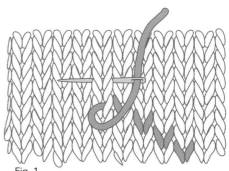

Fig. 1

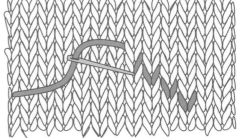

Fig. 2

Single Crochet

Insert hook in stitch indicated, YO and pull up a loop, YO and draw through both loops on hook (Fig. 3) (single crochet made, abbreviated sc).

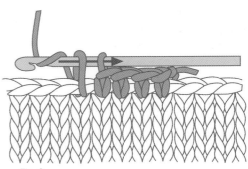

Fig. 3

acknowledgements

Working on this book has been a real joy as well as a huge challenge, but sometimes you just have to step out of your comfort zone and take on that new challenge. For the first time, I not only designed all the projects but I have actually packaged the book. That is, I was able to take charge of the book layout, photography, styling—everything—beginning to end. It has been a huge learning curve for me but I have to say I am extremely proud of the look and feel of this book.

As always, I have many people to thank who helped pull this book together. First I have to give a huge thank you to my editor/stylist and chief baby wrangler Heather Vantress. She has an amazing eye for detail and brought the entire book together with her brilliant styling. To Silvana Di Franco, my incredible photographer, who was able to shoot great photos with wiggling babies. My deepest gratitude to Rita Sowins, book designer extraordinaire, for the beautiful design and layout of this book and for holding my hand through this entire process.

A special thank you to Sandi Rosner for her expert tech editing and support; I know it wasn't always easy to decipher my notes. To Bonnie Reardon and Lee Gant for perfect knitting and pattern writing—couldn't have done it without you. My sample knitter Lene Prior for great work on short notice and to Pam Marshall and her wonderful yarn shop Balls and Skeins in Sebastopol, California.

The wonderful moms and babies; Michele Van Nuys and Evan, Chloe Caviness and Gianna, Amber Distasi and Scarlett, Gloria Ehyai and Zoe, and Amy Pierce and Trevor, I can't thank you enough for having such beautiful children.

My husband who makes me laugh, especially when I'm ready to cry from exhaustion, and all my friends who put up with way too many last minute changes because "I'm finishing a project"—what would I do without you? Last, but certainly not least, to Susan Sullivan and everyone at Leisure Arts, thank you for believing in me and giving me the chance to make this book.